DIGITAL MARKETING TRENDS
FOR BUSINESS GROWTH

Strategies To Elevate Your
Business In 2024

John Dollar

Copyright © 2024

by

John dollar

Table of content

Introduction

Once upon a time, in the bustling city of Technopolis, there lived a young and ambitious individual named Alex Turner. With a keen interest in technology and a knack for creativity, Alex found himself drawn to the ever-evolving world of digital marketing.

Fresh out of university, armed with a degree in marketing and a passion to stay ahead of the curve in the digital landscape, Alex landed a job at startup InnovateHub. This company was known for its cutting-edge approach to business growth, combining traditional marketing strategies with the latest digital trends.

Alex's journey into the field of digital marketing began with an understanding of the basic principles of this field. The startup emphasized the importance of data-driven decision-making, and Alex immersed himself in analytics, learning to decipher trends, customer behavior and market dynamics. Armed with this knowledge, they began developing targeted marketing campaigns that resonated with audiences.

One of the first challenges Alex faced was the shift towards mobile marketing. The team at InnovateHub recognized the growing dependence on smartphones and mobile devices, prompting Alex to focus on creating mobile-friendly content and optimizing campaigns for a seamless mobile experience. Thanks to this initiative, they have seen a significant increase in user engagement and conversion rates.

As the digital landscape has continued to evolve, so has the importance of social media. Alex has immersed himself in creating compelling content for multiple platforms and understands the nuances of each channel. They created visually appealing posts for Instagram, had meaningful conversations on Twitter and harnessed the power of LinkedIn for B2B marketing. The social media efforts not only increased brand visibility, but also fostered a sense of community around the products and services offered by InnovateHub.

Amid digital marketing trends, video content has emerged as a powerful tool. Realizing this, Alex spearheaded the creation of engaging video content, from informative product demos to behind-the-scenes looks at the InnovateHub team. The videos were strategically shared on platforms like YouTube and TikTok, attracting a diverse audience and expanding the brand's reach.

In pursuit of innovation, InnovateHub has embraced influencer marketing. Alex worked with influencers whose values aligned with the brand and created authentic partnerships that resonated with their followers. Influencers brought a human touch to the brand and shared their experiences with InnovateHub products and services. This approach not only expanded the customer base but also built trust and credibility in the market.

As the world became increasingly connected, Alex recognized the importance of harnessing the power of data and artificial intelligence. By implementing AI-driven marketing automation tools, they optimized the customer journey and delivered personalized experiences at every touchpoint. This not only saved time and resources, but also ensured that every interaction with the brand was tailored to the individual consumer.

In the midst of these digital strategies, Alex never lost sight of the importance of storytelling. Realizing that customers connect more deeply with brands that tell compelling stories, they incorporated storytelling into marketing campaigns. Whether it's highlighting a company's origins, showcasing customer success stories, or sharing a team's journey, storytelling has become a powerful tool to humanize a brand and create emotional connections.

However, the field of digital marketing has not been without challenges. The ever-changing algorithms of search engines and social media platforms presented a constant conundrum. Alex navigated this dynamic environment by keeping abreast of the latest updates, quickly adapting strategies and maintaining a flexible approach to marketing campaigns.

InnovateHub's success in digital marketing trends has not only been attributed to the strategies implemented, but also to the culture of continuous learning fostered within the company. Regular workshops, webinars and joint meetings kept the team up-to-date on new technologies and industry best practices. This commitment to staying ahead has ensured that InnovateHub remains a trendsetter in the competitive digital landscape. As time passed, Alex witnessed the tangible results of their efforts. InnovateHub has experienced significant business growth and expanded its customer base worldwide. Innovative digital marketing strategies have not only driven sales, but also established InnovateHub as a thought leader in the industry.

Alex's journey in digital marketing has demonstrated the transformative power of staying on top of trends, embracing innovation and fostering a culture of continuous learning. In the ever-evolving environment of Technopolis, where digital trends shaped the future of businesses, Alex and InnovateHub stood as a testament to the success that can be achieved through strategic, creative and adaptive digital marketing. And so the story of Alex's triumph in digital marketing became an inspiration for budding marketers in the dynamic world of business growth.

Digital marketing is a dynamic and ever-evolving landscape that plays a key role in shaping the success of businesses in today's world. As we delve into the realm of digital marketing trends for business growth, it is imperative to be aware of the rapid transformations that continue to shape the way companies communicate with their audiences, build brand presence and grow revenue. In this survey, we'll walk through the key digital marketing trends that have come to the fore and are poised to shape the future of business strategies.

One leading trend that has gained considerable attention is the rise of artificial intelligence (AI) and machine learning in digital marketing. These technologies have revolutionized the way businesses analyze data, customize user experiences, and automate marketing processes. AI-driven analytics enable organizations to derive actionable insights from vast datasets, providing a comprehensive understanding of consumer behavior and preferences. By leveraging machine learning algorithms, businesses can optimize their marketing campaigns in real-time for a more personalized and effective approach.

In the era of digital communication, the importance of engaging content cannot be overstated. Video content in particular has emerged as a dominant force in digital marketing strategies. With platforms like YouTube, TikTok and Instagram Reels gaining massive popularity, businesses are increasingly using video content to capture the attention of their target audience. The visual appeal of videos not only facilitates storytelling, but also improves brand recall. As a result, businesses are devoting significant resources to creating compelling and shareable video content that resonates with their audiences.

Social media continues to be the cornerstone of digital marketing efforts, but the landscape is constantly evolving. The emergence of new platforms and evolving user preferences on existing ones require a dynamic approach. For example, influencer marketing has become a powerful force in social media strategy, with brands partnering with influencers to leverage their engaged and loyal following. Additionally, the growing importance of social commerce is blurring the lines between social media platforms and online marketplaces. Businesses are integrating seamless shopping into their social media channels, allowing users to shop directly from their favorite platforms.

The shift towards a mobile approach is another key trend in digital marketing. As the majority of Internet users access content through smartphones, businesses prioritize mobile-friendly websites and optimize their campaigns for mobile platforms. Mobile apps have become an integral part of the customer experience, offering convenience, personalization and better user engagement. As mobile usage continues to grow, businesses that neglect mobile optimization risk missing out on a significant portion of their target audience.

The advent of 5G technology is set to further amplify the impact of mobile-focused strategies. The increased speed and connectivity promised by 5G will enable richer multimedia experiences and support innovation in augmented reality (AR) and virtual reality (VR) applications. Marketers are exploring these immersive technologies to create interactive and memorable experiences that take brand engagement to new heights. Whether it's virtual product testing or augmented reality advertising, businesses are using these technologies to deliver unique and engaging customer experiences.

Personalization has long been a key tenet of effective marketing and has evolved to unprecedented levels in the digital age. Consumers expect a personalized experience across all touchpoints, and businesses are responding by leveraging data-driven insights to deliver customized content, recommendations and offers. Machine learning algorithms play a key role in deciphering consumer preferences, enabling businesses to create hyper-personalized marketing strategies that resonate with individual needs and preferences.

The field of personal data protection is undergoing significant changes and consumers are increasingly aware of their data and how it is used. Developments in data protection regulations such as GDPR and CCPA underscore the importance of transparent and ethical data practices. Businesses that prioritize privacy and embrace transparent communication about data usage build trust with their audience and foster stronger customer relationships.

The digital marketing landscape is a dynamic ecosystem where staying ahead of trends is essential for sustained business growth. The integration of artificial intelligence, the dominance of video content, the evolution of social media, mobile access, the impact of 5G, the rise of personalization and the focus on data privacy are all shaping the future of digital marketing. Businesses that embrace these trends and adapt their strategies accordingly are poised to not only survive but thrive in the competitive digital marketplace. As we navigate this ever-changing terrain, the ability to innovate and stay in tune with new trends will continue to be a driving force for businesses looking to harness the full potential of digital marketing foMarketing

Overview of Digital Marketing

Digital marketing is a dynamic field that plays a vital role in the growth and success of businesses in today's digital era. As technology continues to evolve, so do digital marketing trends. Understanding these trends is essential for businesses looking to stay competitive and maximize their online presence.

Introduction to Digital Marketing:

Digital marketing encompasses a wide range of online channels and strategies designed to connect businesses with their target audience. From search engine optimization (SEO) and social media marketing to email campaigns and content creation, businesses use digital platforms to reach and engage customers.

Current Digital Marketing Landscape:

In recent years, several trends have emerged that have reshaped the digital marketing landscape. One of the significant trends is the increased emphasis on user experience. Websites and digital content are now designed with a focus on providing a seamless and enjoyable experience for users. This not only increases customer satisfaction, but also positively affects search engine rankings.

Search Engine Optimization (SEO):

SEO continues to be the cornerstone of digital marketing. As search engines are constantly improving their algorithms, it is essential for businesses to stay up-to-date on SEO best practices. Voice search optimization, mobile-first indexing and featured snippets are some of the key areas within SEO that businesses need to consider in order to gain an effective online presence.

Content Marketing:

Content remains king in digital marketing. However, the focus has shifted towards creating high-quality and valuable content that resonates with target audiences. Video content is coming to the fore and platforms like YouTube and TikTok are becoming essential to reach younger demographics. Interactive content such as quizzes and polls is also on the rise to provide engaging experiences for users.

Social Media Marketing:

Social media platforms continue to be powerful tools for businesses to connect with their audiences. Instagram, Facebook, Twitter and LinkedIn remain popular choices, but new platforms should not be ignored. The trend is towards authentic and relatable content, with influencers playing a significant role in brand promotion. In addition, there is a growing use of social commerce, which allows users to make purchases directly through social media platforms.

Email Marketing and Automation:
Email marketing remains a cost-effective way to generate leads and retain customers. Personalization and automation are key trends in this area. Businesses use data to deliver targeted and relevant content to their audience, enhancing the overall customer experience. Automated workflows streamline processes, save time and ensure timely communication.

Privacy and Security:
With data privacy concerns on the rise, businesses must prioritize the security of customer information. Implementing strict data protection measures and transparent privacy policies is essential. This not only builds trust with customers but also ensures compliance with regulations such as GDPR.

Artificial Intelligence (AI) and Machine Learning:

Artificial intelligence and machine learning are transforming digital marketing by providing insights and automating tasks. Chatbots, personalized recommendations and predictive analytics are becoming an integral part of marketing strategies. Artificial intelligence allows businesses to analyze vast amounts of data, enabling more informed decision-making and targeted marketing campaigns.

An overview of digital marketing reveals a landscape that is constantly evolving. Keeping up with these trends is essential to achieve business growth. Businesses must adapt their strategies to align with the changing digital marketing landscape, embrace new technologies and customer-centric approaches. As we move forward, the integration of these trends will shape the future of digital marketing, presenting both challenges and opportunities for businesses striving to thrive in the digital age.

Definition and Scope of Digital Marketing

Digital marketing is a dynamic and vast field that plays a key role in the growth of businesses in today's digital age. At its core, digital marketing involves using various online channels and platforms to promote products, services or brands. The scope of digital marketing is broad and includes a number of strategies and techniques that use the power of the Internet to reach and engage target audiences. In this article, we will delve into the definition and scope of digital marketing and highlight its importance in the context of new trends that contribute to business growth.

Definition of Digital Marketing:
Digital marketing refers to the use of digital channels such as search engines, social media, email, websites and online advertising to connect with current and potential customers. Unlike traditional marketing, digital marketing uses the Internet's vast reach and interactive capabilities to create targeted and measurable campaigns. It

includes various components, including search engine optimization (SEO), content marketing, social media marketing, email marketing and paid advertising, all working together to achieve marketing goals.

Scope of Digital Marketing:

The scope of digital marketing is vast and covers a wide range of activities that businesses can use to create an online presence, build brand awareness and drive customer engagement. Let's explore some of the key components of a digital marketing landscape:

1. Search Engine Optimization (SEO): SEO is a fundamental aspect of digital marketing that focuses on optimizing a website's visibility in search engine results. By using SEO best practices, businesses can improve their rankings, leading to increased organic traffic and better online visibility.

2. Content Marketing: Content is king in the digital realm. Content marketing involves creating and distributing valuable, relevant and consistent

content to attract and retain a target audience. High-quality content not only engages users, but also contributes to SEO efforts and brand authority.

3. Social Media Marketing: Social media platforms serve as powerful tools for connecting with audiences. Social media marketing involves creating and sharing content on platforms such as Facebook, Instagram, Twitter, and LinkedIn to build brand awareness, drive engagement, and drive traffic to a business's website.

4. Email Marketing: Email remains an effective channel for communication and marketing. Email marketing involves sending targeted messages to a list of subscribers to promote products, share updates, and maintain customer relationships.

5. Paid Advertising: Digital advertising allows businesses to reach specific demographics through targeted ads. Platforms like Google Ads, Facebook Ads, and Instagram Ads allow businesses to serve ads to users based on their interests, behaviors, and demographics.

Digital Marketing Trends for Business Growth:
To remain competitive in a rapidly evolving digital environment, businesses must adapt to new trends. Several trends are currently shaping the digital marketing landscape and contributing to business growth:

1. Personalization: Tailoring marketing messages to individual preferences improves user experience and increases engagement. Personalization is achieved through data analytics, which enables businesses to deliver relevant content and offers to their target audience.

2. Video Marketing: The popularity of video content continues to grow. Businesses use cross-platform video marketing to deliver messages, showcase products and connect with audiences on a more personal level.

3. Voice Search Optimization: With the proliferation of voice-activated devices, optimizing content for voice search becomes essential. Businesses must

adapt their digital marketing strategies to accommodate the growing trend of voice-activated search.

4. Artificial Intelligence (AI) and Chatbots: AI-driven technologies like chatbots are changing customer interactions. Chatbots provide instant responses, streamline customer service and contribute to a personalized user experience.

5. Ephemeral Content: Platforms like Snapchat and Instagram Stories have popularized ephemeral content. Businesses use these short-term and engaging formats to create a sense of urgency and foster a more authentic connection with their audience.

The definition and scope of digital marketing encompasses a diverse range of strategies aimed at leveraging online channels for business growth. Keeping up with new trends is essential for businesses that want to leverage the full potential of digital marketing and remain competitive in today's digital environment. By embracing these trends and adapting their strategies accordingly, businesses can drive brand growth, connect with target audiences and thrive in the dynamic world of digital marketing.

Evolution of Digital Marketing Strategies

Digital marketing has undergone a profound evolution in recent years, shaped by dynamic trends that have redefined the landscape for businesses seeking growth. This development is crucial for companies trying to stay ahead in an increasingly competitive online environment. In this exploration of the evolution of digital marketing strategies, we'll delve into the key trends that have impacted the industry and discuss their implications for business growth.

1. The Rise of Social Media Marketing:

Social media has become a cornerstone of digital marketing strategies. Platforms like Facebook, Instagram, Twitter and LinkedIn have transformed from mere social networks to powerful marketing tools. Businesses use these platforms to reach their audience, build brand awareness and increase traffic to their website.

2. Moving towards content marketing:

Content is king in the digital realm. The emphasis on quality content has grown significantly and businesses have understood the value of providing valuable and relevant information to their audience. Content marketing not only increases brand authority, but also contributes to search engine optimization (SEO), a vital aspect of any successful digital strategy.

3. Mobile access:

The proliferation of smartphones has led to a mobile approach in digital marketing. With a significant portion of internet users accessing content on mobile devices, businesses have adapted their strategies to ensure a seamless mobile experience. Responsive design, mobile-friendly content, and targeted mobile advertising have become essential for success.

4. Dominance of video marketing:

Video content is becoming increasingly popular with the rise of platforms like YouTube and the integration of social media video features. Businesses are capitalizing on this trend by creating engaging video content to tell their brand stories, showcase products and connect with audiences on a more personal level.

5. Personalization and AI Integration:

Personalized marketing experiences have become the norm with the integration of artificial intelligence (AI) technologies. Machine learning algorithms analyze user behavior and deliver customized content, recommendations and ads. This personalization not only increases user satisfaction, but also increases the likelihood of conversion.

6. Influencer marketing:

Working with influencers has proven to be an effective strategy for businesses to reach a wider audience. With their established credibility and large following, influencers can effectively promote products or services and lend authenticity to a brand's message.

7. Transient Content and Stories:

The popularity of ephemeral content like Instagram Stories and Snapchat Snaps has changed the way businesses approach content creation. These engaging, short-lived formats allow brands to connect with their audiences in a more spontaneous and authentic way, fostering a sense of immediacy and exclusivity.

8. Voice Search Optimization:

The rise of voice-activated devices and virtual assistants has led to content being optimized for voice search. Businesses are adapting their SEO strategies to accommodate the conversational nature of voice search and ensure their content remains relevant and accessible.

9. Privacy and Compliance Concerns:

Growing privacy concerns have prompted more stringent regulations such as GDPR and CCPA. Businesses must prioritize ethical and transparent data practices to build trust with their audience. Adherence to these regulations is not only a legal requirement, but also necessary to maintain a positive brand image.

10. Integration of Augmented Reality (AR) and Virtual Reality (VR):

AR and VR technologies are gradually finding their place in digital marketing. Businesses are exploring innovative ways to use AR and VR for immersive brand experiences, product demonstrations and virtual storefronts.

The development of digital marketing strategies is intrinsically linked to the ever-changing environment of the online world. Businesses that adapt to these trends and embrace new technologies will not only survive, but thrive in the digital era. As we move forward, staying informed and agile will be paramount for companies seeking sustained growth in a competitive digital marketplace.

Importance of Staying Updated with Trends

Staying informed about digital marketing trends is paramount for businesses seeking sustained growth in today's dynamic environment. As technology evolves and consumer behavior undergoes constant change, it becomes a strategic imperative to stay ahead. Here's an in-depth look at why keeping up with digital marketing trends is critical to business success.

First, understanding the latest trends allows businesses to align their strategies with changing consumer preferences. In the digital realm, consumer behavior is influenced by a number of factors, from technological advances to cultural shifts. By staying current, businesses can tailor their marketing approaches to resonate with their target audience, increasing engagement and conversion rates.

Additionally, staying informed about new technologies allows businesses to adopt innovative tools and platforms. For example, the rise of augmented reality (AR) and virtual reality (VR) has opened new avenues for immersive marketing experiences. By incorporating such technologies, businesses can differentiate themselves and create memorable interactions that set them apart from the competition.

In the fast-paced world of digital marketing, search engine optimization (SEO) algorithms and criteria change frequently. Keeping up with these changes ensures that businesses maintain or improve their online visibility. Regular updates to search engine algorithms allow marketers to adjust their content strategies and ensure their website ranks high on search engine results pages (SERPs), which in turn increases organic traffic.

Additionally, the ability to anticipate and respond to industry trends is critical to staying relevant. In digital marketing, trends can emerge quickly and have a significant impact. By staying current, businesses can proactively adjust their strategies and avoid the risk of becoming obsolete or losing market share to more agile competitors.

Social media platforms are an integral part of digital marketing and their algorithms are constantly evolving. Being aware of these changes is critical to optimizing your social media marketing efforts. For example, understanding algorithm updates on platforms like Instagram or Facebook allows businesses to tailor their content strategies to maximize visibility and engagement, ultimately increasing brand awareness and customer loyalty.

The digital landscape is also heavily influenced by data and analytics. Keeping up with the latest data analysis tools and methodologies ensures that businesses can gain meaningful insights from their campaigns. This in turn enables data-driven decision-making, allowing marketers to efficiently allocate resources and refine their strategies based on real-time performance metrics.

Another critical aspect of constantly monitoring digital marketing trends is the opportunity for early adoption. Being among the first to adopt a new trend or technology gives businesses a competitive advantage. Early adopters often enjoy greater visibility, increased credibility, and a chance to gain more market share before saturation occurs.

Moreover, the digital space is interconnected, with trends in one area often influencing others. Staying current allows businesses to identify opportunities across channels. For example, an emerging trend in content marketing can complement and increase the effectiveness of an existing email marketing strategy. By recognizing these synergies, businesses can create integrated, cohesive campaigns that amplify their impact.

Customer expectations are constantly evolving, and digital marketing trends often reflect these changes. Staying current helps businesses stay in tune with customer preferences, allowing them to provide a more personalized and relevant experience. This customer-centric approach fosters stronger relationships, increases customer satisfaction and ultimately contributes to long-term brand loyalty.

The importance of constantly monitoring digital marketing trends cannot be overstated. It is a dynamic area where adaptation and innovation are the keys to success. Businesses that prioritize awareness are positioning themselves to not only survive in an ever-evolving digital landscape, but also thrive by seizing new opportunities and meeting the evolving expectations of their target audience.

Chapter 1: Evolving Landscape of Digital Marketing

Digital marketing, once a peripheral aspect of business strategy, has now become a cornerstone for organizations that want to thrive in the digital age. The digital marketing landscape is dynamic and trends are constantly shaping the way businesses connect with their audiences, drive engagement and ultimately drive growth. In this survey, we dive into the key digital marketing trends that are impacting the business landscape and discuss how companies can leverage these trends to achieve sustainable growth.

1. Personalization: The Power of Tailored Experiences:
Personalization has emerged as a key trend in digital marketing, redefining the way brands interact with their audiences. Consumers are inundated with information on a daily basis, so it's critical for businesses to cut through the noise and deliver

personalized experiences. By leveraging AI-driven data analytics and insights, companies can create targeted content, recommendations and ads that resonate with individual preferences. This customized approach not only increases customer satisfaction, but also promotes brand loyalty and increases conversion rates.

2. Video Dominance: Grabbing Attention in Seconds

Video content has become the undisputed king of digital marketing, with platforms like YouTube, TikTok and Instagram playing a major role. Short videos, in particular, have gained huge popularity and allow businesses to convey their message succinctly and engage their audience with visually compelling content. As attention spans continue to shrink, the ability to grab and hold attention within seconds is a key skill for marketers. Incorporating video into marketing strategies can significantly increase brand visibility and customer engagement.

3. Voice Search Optimization: Adapting to Changing Search Behavior:

The rise of voice-activated devices such as smart speakers and virtual assistants has led to a shift in search behavior. People are increasingly using voice commands to search for information, and businesses need to optimize their online presence accordingly. Optimizing voice search involves tailoring content to match natural language queries, as users tend to phrase voice searches differently than typed queries. By embracing this trend, businesses can improve their online visibility and ensure they remain discoverable in the evolving search landscape.

4. Interactive Content: Engaging Your Audience Through Participation:

Interactive content goes beyond traditional static posts and encourages users to actively engage with the material. Polls, quizzes, surveys and interactive infographics are just a few examples of how businesses can engage their audience. This form of content not only increases user engagement but also provides valuable data insights. By creating interactive experiences, companies can foster a sense of engagement and connection and build a deeper relationship with their audience.

5. Social commerce: seamless shopping in social spaces:

The integration of e-commerce into social media platforms gave rise to social commerce. Platforms like Instagram and Facebook now allow users to discover, research and buy products without leaving the app. This trend benefits from the social aspect of online shopping as users can share their purchases, recommendations and reviews with their network. For businesses, social commerce offers a direct path to turning social media engagement into tangible sales, streamlining the customer journey and increasing revenue.

6. AI and Machine Learning: Data-Driven Decision Making:

Artificial intelligence (AI) and machine learning (ML) are changing the digital marketing landscape by enabling data-driven decision-making processes. From predictive analytics to customer segmentation, artificial intelligence enables marketers to effectively analyze vast data sets. This enables more precise targeting, personalized recommendations and automatic campaign optimization. As businesses continue to collect data, leveraging the power of AI and ML becomes imperative to remain competitive in the digital marketplace.

7.Augmented Reality (AR) in Marketing: Immersive Experiences:

Augmented reality creates immersive experiences that bridge the gap between the virtual and physical worlds. Brands are incorporating AR into their marketing strategies to provide interactive and engaging experiences for customers. From virtual fitting experiences for fashion brands to AR-enabled product demonstrations, this technology is improving consumer interaction and helping businesses stand out in a crowded digital space. As AR technology becomes more accessible, its incorporation into marketing campaigns is expected to increase.

8. Inclusive Marketing: Embracing Diversity and Authenticity:

At a time when consumers value authenticity, inclusive marketing has come to the fore. Brands recognize the importance of representing diverse perspectives in their advertising and promotional efforts. This is not only in line with societal values but also resonates with a wider audience. Companies that authentically embrace inclusivity are more likely to build trust with their audience and create a positive brand image.

9. Privacy and Transparency: Building Trust in the Digital Sphere:

With data privacy concerns on the rise, transparency has become a critical part of successful digital marketing strategies. Consumers want to know how their data is being used, and businesses that prioritize transparent communication build trust with their audience. Complying with data protection regulations, clearly communicating privacy policies and obtaining user consent are essential steps for businesses navigating the evolving privacy landscape.

10. Adapting to the Metaverse: A New Frontier for Marketing:

The concept of meta version, a collective virtual shared space, is gaining momentum and presents new opportunities for digital marketing. Brands are exploring ways to make themselves visible in virtual worlds to create immersive experiences and interactions. While the metaverse is still in its infancy, forward-thinking businesses are beginning to explore its potential for marketing and customer engagement, envisioning a future where virtual experiences will play a significant role in brand interactions.

Navigating the seas of digital marketing:

The digital marketing landscape is a vast and ever-changing terrain that requires businesses to constantly adapt. Staying ahead of trends and adopting innovative strategies is essential for organizations seeking sustained growth in the digital age. From personalized experiences to immersive technologies, the key is to understand evolving consumer needs and leverage digital marketing trends to create meaningful connections. Like a road through a trench

1.1 Historical Perspective

In a dynamic business and marketing environment, understanding the historical context of digital marketing trends is critical to navigating the ever-evolving strategies that drive growth. Over the years, the evolution of digital marketing has reflected and often catalyzed changes in technology, consumer behavior and market dynamics. Examining the historical path provides valuable insights into the forces shaping today's trends and offers a blueprint for businesses seeking effective strategies to drive growth.

Emergence of Digital Marketing:
The roots of digital marketing can be traced back to the early days of the Internet. As the World Wide Web gained popularity in the 1990s, businesses recognized the potential to reach global audiences through online channels. The initial focus was on building a digital presence, with websites serving as the primary tool for online visibility. During this era,

the basic practices of search engine optimization (SEO) emerged as businesses sought to improve the visibility of their websites in search engines.

The Rise of Search Engines and SEO:

With the advent of search engines like Yahoo and AltaVista, businesses began to understand the importance of optimizing their websites to rank higher in search results. This marked the birth of SEO as a core digital marketing strategy. Companies have been racing to incorporate relevant keywords, meta tags and other SEO techniques to improve their online visibility.

The Social Media Revolution:

The early 21st century saw the rise of social media platforms that transformed the digital landscape. Friendster, MySpace, and eventually Facebook opened up new ways for businesses to connect with their audiences on a more personal level. The shift from one-way communication to interactive engagement has changed marketing strategies. Brands have started using social media to build communities, share content and cultivate brand loyalty.

Content Marketing Takes Center Stage:
As the digital ecosystem has matured, content marketing has emerged as a powerful force. Instead of just promoting products, businesses have started focusing on creating valuable and relevant content to attract and engage their target audience. Blogging has become a popular tool for sharing industry insights, thought leadership and deeper connections with customers.

Mobile Optimization and the Rise of Smartphones:
The mid-2000s saw a significant shift with the widespread adoption of smartphones. This transition has forced businesses to adapt their digital marketing strategies to accommodate mobile users. Mobile optimization has become critical, responsive web design and mobile-friendly content have become standard practices. Marketers have started incorporating location-based services and mobile apps to improve the customer experience.

The era of data-driven marketing:

Advances in technology have brought large amounts of data. The ability to track and analyze user behavior has enabled marketers to make more informed decisions. The rise of data analytics tools has allowed businesses to improve targeting, personalize messaging and measure the effectiveness of their campaigns with unprecedented precision.

Impact of Artificial Intelligence and Machine Learning:

In recent years, artificial intelligence (AI) and machine learning have become an integral part of digital marketing. These technologies allow businesses to automate processes, personalize user experiences, and optimize advertising campaigns in real time. Predictive analytics and chatbots are examples of how artificial intelligence is transforming customer interactions and increasing the effectiveness of marketing efforts.

Development of e-commerce and Omnichannel Marketing:

The constant growth of e-commerce has changed the way businesses approach marketing. The convenience of online shopping along with advances in payment gateways and security have led to an increase in digital transactions. Omnichannel marketing, which seamlessly integrates different channels, has become essential to deliver a cohesive and immersive customer experience across online and offline touchpoints.

Current trends shaping digital marketing:
Looking to the present, several trends are shaping the digital marketing landscape. Influencer marketing, video content, interactive experiences and sustainability initiatives are coming to the fore. Additionally, the emphasis on user-generated content and the growing importance of voice search are influencing the way businesses communicate with their audiences.

In the great tapestry of digital marketing, understanding its historical development is crucial for businesses that want to thrive in today's competitive environment. From the beginnings of websites and SEO to the current era of AI-driven strategies, this journey highlights the adaptability and innovation that are part of successful marketing approaches. As we stand at the intersection of technology and consumer behavior, businesses that take a historical perspective will be better equipped to navigate the ever-changing currents of digital marketing and drive sustainable growth in the future.

1.2 Current Trends Shaping the Industry

In the ever-evolving realm of digital marketing, staying ahead of trends is key for businesses seeking sustainable growth. As we delve into the current environment, several trends are shaping the industry and influencing strategies for businesses looking to thrive in the digital realm.

1. Rise of Artificial Intelligence (AI) and Machine Learning (ML):

AI and ML are revolutionizing digital marketing by enhancing personalization and automation. From chatbots offering real-time customer support to predictive analytics optimizing ad targeting, businesses are using AI to streamline processes and deliver personalized experiences.

2. Dominance of video content:

Video continues to be a dominant force in digital marketing. Short videos on platforms like TikTok and Reels grab users' attention, while live streaming encourages real-time engagement. Businesses are increasingly incorporating video content into their strategies to connect with audiences on a more emotional level.

3. Voice Search Optimization:

The prevalence of voice-activated devices has led to an increase in voice search. Businesses are adapting their SEO strategies to suit conversational queries and ensure they remain visible in voice search results. This shift highlights the importance of natural language and long-tail keywords.

4. Transient Social Media Content:

The popularity of stories on platforms like Instagram and Snapchat highlights the appeal of ephemeral content. Businesses are capitalizing on this trend by creating time-sensitive and engaging content that fosters a sense of urgency and exclusivity in their viewers.

5. Social Commerce Integration:
Social media platforms are evolving into powerful sales channels. With features like Instagram Shopping and Facebook Marketplace, businesses can seamlessly integrate ecommerce into social platforms, reducing friction in the customer journey and improving the overall shopping experience.

6. Privacy and data protection:
As privacy regulations tighten, businesses must prioritize ethical data practices. With the implementation of measures such as cookie-free tracking and explicit consent mechanisms, marketers are adapting their strategies to maintain consumer trust while delivering personalized experiences.

7. Augmented Reality (AR) Experiences:
AR is changing the way consumers interact with brands. From virtual fitting experiences in the

fashion industry to interactive product demos, businesses are incorporating AR to increase engagement and deliver immersive experiences that set them apart from the competition.

8. The evolution of influencer marketing:

Influencer marketing continues to evolve, with a shift towards authenticity and niche influence. Micro-influencers with smaller but highly engaged audiences are gaining in importance as businesses recognize the value of real connections and targeted reach.

In the fast-paced world of digital marketing, adapting to trends is essential for business growth. Embracing artificial intelligence, prioritizing video content, optimizing for voice search, leveraging ephemeral content, integrating social commerce, addressing privacy concerns, exploring AR, and evolving influencer marketing strategies are all key steps to staying relevant and competitive.

As businesses navigate this dynamic landscape, a holistic approach that combines these trends with a deep understanding of target audiences will undoubtedly pave the way for sustained digital success.

1.3 Impact of Technological Advancements

In the rapidly evolving landscape of digital marketing, technological advancements play a key role in shaping the trends that drive business growth. As businesses increasingly use digital channels to connect with their audiences, it becomes imperative to keep up with technological changes. This article explores the profound impact of technological advancements on digital marketing trends and how businesses can leverage these changes for sustained growth.

1. Data Driven Decision Making:
Technological advances have ushered in an era of unprecedented data availability. Big data analytics and artificial intelligence (AI) have enabled businesses to make informed decisions based on comprehensive insights. By analyzing consumer behavior, preferences and market trends,

businesses can tailor their digital marketing strategies with unparalleled precision. This data-driven approach not only improves targeting, but also ensures a more personalized and engaging customer experience.

2. Personalization and Customer Experience:
Advances in technology have given rise to highly personalized marketing strategies. Machine learning algorithms allow businesses to understand the preferences and behavior of individual customers and enable the creation of targeted and relevant content. Personalized experiences, whether through tailored recommendations or dynamic content, foster a stronger connection between brands and consumers. This personalization not only increases customer satisfaction, but also contributes to increased brand loyalty and advocacy.

#3. Automation and Efficiency:
Automation has revolutionized digital marketing processes, greatly improving efficiency and scalability. Tasks such as email marketing, social

media posting and ad campaign management can now be automated, freeing up time for marketers to focus on strategy and creativity. Marketing automation tools allow businesses to streamline their workflows, reduce manual errors, and ensure consistent and timely communication with audiences. This efficiency not only saves resources, but also enables a more agile response to market dynamics.

4. Emergence of chatbots and conversational marketing:

Conversational marketing has come to the fore with the rise of AI-driven chatbots. These bots facilitate real-time interactions, provide immediate responses to customer inquiries, and guide them through the sales funnel. A conversational approach increases user engagement, provides immediate assistance and creates a more interactive brand experience. As technology continues to improve natural language processing, chatbots are becoming more sophisticated and contributing to a seamless and personalized customer journey.

5. Dominance of video marketing:

Technological advancements in internet speed and mobile devices have pushed video content to the forefront of digital marketing. Live broadcasts, 360° videos and interactive content are changing the way brands communicate with their audiences. Video marketing not only attracts attention more effectively, but also fosters an emotional connection. By integrating augmented reality (AR) and virtual reality (VR), businesses can create immersive and memorable experiences that further enhance their digital presence and brand perception.

6. Evolving SEO Strategy:

Search engine optimization (SEO) strategies are constantly evolving in response to technological changes. Voice search, mobile optimization, and AI-driven search algorithms have changed the way businesses approach SEO. Optimizing for voice-activated devices and ensuring a mobile experience have become essential to maintaining search visibility. Understanding and adapting to these technological shifts is essential for businesses that want to remain competitive in the digital environment.

7. Blockchain technology in digital advertising: Blockchain technology is disrupting traditional digital advertising models. By providing transparent and decentralized systems, blockchain solves the problems of fraud, misplacement and lack of accountability. Smart contracts on blockchain platforms enable more accurate tracking of ad performance and ensure that advertisers get value for their investment. As blockchain adoption grows, businesses can expect increased trust and reliability in their digital advertising efforts.

Technological advancements are reshaping the digital marketing landscape at a rapid pace. Businesses that embrace these changes and adapt their strategies accordingly will gain a competitive advantage in the evolving digital marketplace. From data-driven decision making to personalized customer experiences, automation and the integration of emerging technologies, the impact of technology on digital marketing is profound. Staying informed and agile in adopting these improvements is critical for businesses seeking sustained growth in an ever-changing digital landscape.

Chapter 2: Content Marketing Strategies

In the ever-evolving digital marketing landscape, businesses are constantly looking for innovative ways to connect with their target audience and drive growth. Content marketing has proven to be an effective strategy that blends seamlessly with digital marketing trends to create a dynamic approach to business expansion. This article explores the symbiotic relationship between content marketing strategies and current digital marketing trends and how businesses can leverage these synergies for sustained growth.

1. Understanding Content Marketing:
Content marketing involves creating and distributing valuable, relevant and consistent content to attract and engage a target audience. The main purpose is to build trust, establish

authority and ultimately drive profitable customer actions. In the digital realm, this can include various forms of content, including blog posts, videos, infographics, podcasts and social media posts.

2. SEO integration:

One of the key digital marketing trends shaping business growth is the ever-increasing importance of search engine optimization (SEO). Content marketing and SEO are interconnected strategies that complement each other. High quality and relevant content improves website visibility in search engine results, increases organic traffic and improves rankings. As search engines prioritize valuable content, businesses must align their content marketing strategies with SEO best practices to remain competitive in the digital landscape.

3. Dominance of video content:

Video content has seen explosive growth and has become a dominant force in digital marketing. Platforms like YouTube, TikTok and Instagram Reels have revolutionized the way businesses connect with their audiences. Incorporating video content into content marketing strategies provides a dynamic and engaging way to deliver messages, showcase products and build brand identity. Taking advantage of this trend can significantly increase a company's reach and impact in the digital space.

4. Personalization and user experience:

The rise of personalization in digital marketing emphasizes tailoring content to individual preferences and behaviors. Content marketing plays a key role in delivering personalized experiences, whether through personalized email campaigns, targeted content recommendations or interactive website elements. By understanding their audience and creating content that resonates on a personal level, businesses can improve user experience, foster loyalty and increase conversion rates.

5. Social network expansion:

Social media remains the cornerstone of digital marketing, and content is the fuel that drives social engagement. With the widespread use of platforms such as Facebook, Instagram, Twitter and LinkedIn, businesses can expand their content to reach a wider audience. Social media algorithms often favor relevant and engaging content, making it essential for businesses to create compelling stories and visuals that resonate with their target demographic.

6. Voice search optimization:

The growing prevalence of voice-activated devices and virtual assistants has led to the rise of voice search optimization as a critical aspect of digital marketing. Content marketing strategies must adapt to this trend by creating content that aligns with natural language queries. Businesses should focus on creating conversational and informative content to improve their visibility in voice search results and stay ahead of the curve in the evolving digital landscape.

7. Influencer collaborations:

Influencer marketing has become the driving force of digital promotion, and content marketing plays a vital role in successful collaboration. By partnering with influencers relevant to their industry, businesses can leverage existing influencer audiences to amplify their content. Authentic and well-crafted content that is seamlessly integrated into an influencer's platform can increase brand awareness and credibility, contributing to overall business growth.

8. Interactive content engagement:
Interactive content is a rising star in the digital marketing constellation. Polls, quizzes, surveys and interactive infographics attract audience attention and encourage participation. This not only increases user engagement but also provides valuable data insights. Integrating interactive elements into content marketing strategies supports a two-way communication channel and creates an immersive and memorable experience for the audience.

9. Emerging Technologies:
As technologies like augmented reality (AR) and virtual reality (VR) gain traction, businesses are looking for innovative ways to incorporate them into

content marketing. Through AR/VR content, immersive experiences can be created that offer consumers a unique and memorable interaction with a brand. Keeping up with emerging technologies and integrating them into content strategies can give businesses a competitive edge and position them as industry leaders.

10. Data-driven decision making:

The digital age provides businesses with an abundance of data. Content marketing strategies should be based on data-driven insights, analyzing user behavior, preferences and engagement metrics. By understanding what resonates with audiences, businesses can refine their approach to content, optimize campaigns and effectively allocate resources to maximize return on investment.

Synergy between content marketing strategies and digital marketing trends is essential for business growth in the current environment. Adapting to SEO best practices, incorporating video content, personalizing the user experience, leveraging social media, optimizing for voice search, working with influencers, incorporating interactive elements, and keeping up with new technologies are all key components of a holistic and effective content marketing strategy.

Businesses that embrace these trends and align their content marketing efforts with the evolving digital landscape are better positioned to not only survive, but thrive in an increasingly competitive market. As we move forward, the integration of cutting-edge technologies and a commitment to delivering valuable and engaging content will be essential for businesses seeking sustained growth and relevance in the ever-changing world of digital marketing.

2.1 Importance of Content Marketing

In the dynamic digital marketing landscape, businesses are constantly adapting their strategies to stay relevant and competitive. Content marketing has emerged as a key element in this ever-evolving ecosystem, playing a key role in driving engagement, building brand awareness and ultimately driving business growth.

Understanding Content Marketing:

Content marketing is more than just creating and distributing content. It involves creating valuable, relevant and consistent content to attract and retain a clearly defined audience. In a digital age where consumers are bombarded with information, content marketing serves as a strategic approach to cut through the noise and connect with your target audience on a deeper level.

Digital transformation and its impact:

Digital transformation has changed the way businesses operate and communicate with their audiences. With the proliferation of online channels and platforms, consumers now have unprecedented access to information. As a result, traditional advertising methods are losing their effectiveness and businesses are turning to content marketing to deliver messages in a more authentic and meaningful way.

SEO and Content Synergy:

Search Engine Optimization (SEO) is a fundamental aspect of digital marketing, and content marketing and SEO are closely linked. High-quality and relevant content not only attracts human readers, but also satisfies search engine algorithms. Since search engines favor content that provides value to users, businesses investing in content marketing are likely to see better search rankings, increased organic traffic, and improved online visibility.

Building Brand Authority and Trust:
In a digital environment where trust is a valuable commodity, content marketing becomes a powerful tool for building brand authority. By consistently providing valuable and informative content, businesses become industry leaders and experts. This positioning not only attracts potential customers, but also fosters trust, making consumers more likely to choose a brand they perceive to be knowledgeable and trustworthy.

Multi-channel connection:
Digital marketing encompasses a multitude of channels, including social media, email, blogs, and more. Content marketing seamlessly integrates

with these channels, giving businesses a versatile approach to engaging their audience. Whether it's a blog post shared on social media, an informative email newsletter or an engaging video, content marketing allows businesses to connect with their audience through multiple touch points.

Personalization and customer-oriented approach:
One of the significant trends in digital marketing is the shift towards personalization. Consumers today expect personalized experiences, and content marketing enables businesses to meet this demand. With data-driven insights, businesses can tailor their content to specific audience segments and deliver messages that resonate on a personal level. This customer-centric approach not only increases engagement, but also contributes to long-term customer loyalty.

ROI Measurement and Analysis:
In digital marketing, data is king. Content marketing allows businesses to track and measure the performance of their efforts through analytics tools. Whether it's website traffic, conversion rates or

social media engagement, businesses can gather valuable insights to refine their strategies. This data-driven approach not only helps to understand the effectiveness of content, but also provides a basis for continuous improvement.

Staying agile in a dynamic environment:
The digital landscape is characterized by constant evolution. Consumer trends and behavior change, algorithms change and new technologies emerge. With its adaptive nature, content marketing allows businesses to remain agile and responsive. By consistently producing relevant and timely content, businesses can stay ahead and adapt to the changing dynamics of the digital space.

In the rapidly evolving digital marketing landscape, content marketing is a cornerstone for businesses seeking sustainable growth. It's not just a trend, but a strategic imperative to build brand presence, engage audiences and increase conversions. As businesses navigate the complex digital terrain, an integrated approach that combines content marketing with other digital strategies will undoubtedly contribute to long-term success and resilience in a competitive marketplace.

2.2 Video Content Trends

In the ever-evolving digital marketing landscape, video content has emerged as a key force that is changing the way businesses connect with their audiences. As technology and consumer preferences change, keeping up with the latest video content trends is becoming a must for businesses looking to thrive in a competitive online environment. This article explores the key video content trends that are impacting digital marketing strategies and driving business growth.

1. Dominance of short videos
Short videos, epitomized by platforms like TikTok and Instagram Reels, have become the focus of attention. These biting and engaging clips cater to the shrinking attention spans of online audiences. For businesses, creating concise and compelling video content has become an effective way to capture attention, deliver messages quickly, and drive user engagement.

2. Interactive video experiences:

Interactive videos change the user experience. Features like clickables, quizzes and polls embedded in videos turn passive viewers into active participants. Businesses are capitalizing on this trend to create immersive content that not only entertains but also engages audiences, resulting in higher retention and increased brand engagement.

3. Live broadcast for authentic connection;

Live broadcasting has become a tool to interact with the audience in real time. Platforms like Facebook Live and YouTube Live allow businesses to authentically connect with their audience. Live Q&A sessions, behind-the-scenes looks and real-time product launches foster a sense of immediacy and transparency, strengthening the bond between brands and consumers.

4. Personalized and targeted video content:

Personalization is not a new concept, but its integration into video content is on the rise. Businesses use data analytics to tailor video content based on user preferences, demographics and behavior. Personalized videos increase the relevance of content, leading to higher engagement rates and more opportunities to convert.

5. Vertical video format for mobile optimization:

As the use of mobile devices continues to increase, the vertical video format has become the choice for content consumption. This format maximizes the screen size on smartphones and provides a seamless viewing experience. Businesses adapt their video content to this format and ensure that their message resonates effectively with the first generation of mobile devices.

6. Storytelling through video:

Storytelling remains a powerful tool in digital marketing, and video is an ideal vehicle for narrative content. Businesses create compelling stories that resonate emotionally with their audiences. Whether it's showcasing a brand journey or highlighting customer testimonials, storytelling through video fosters a deeper connection with your audience, building trust and loyalty.

7. Artificial intelligence and video creation:

Artificial Intelligence (AI) is making waves in video content creation. AI tools enable businesses to automate video production processes, from generating personalized video recommendations to content editing and optimization. This trend not only saves time, but also opens up new possibilities for dynamic and data-driven video campaigns.

8. Social Commerce Integration:

Video and social commerce are converging to create a seamless shopping experience for consumers. Platforms like Instagram and TikTok integrate shopping features directly into video content, allowing users to make purchases without leaving the app. This presents a powerful opportunity for businesses to convert engagement into sales through shoppable video content.

In the dynamic realm of digital marketing, staying ahead of video content trends is key to business growth. From the rise of short videos to the integration of artificial intelligence into content creation, each trend represents a unique opportunity for businesses to connect with their audiences in a meaningful way. Embracing these video content trends not only improves brand visibility, but also fosters a deeper and more authentic relationship with the ever-evolving digital consumer. As we move into the future of digital marketing, the ability to harness the power of video content will undoubtedly remain a cornerstone of success for businesses looking to thrive in the online arena.

2.3 User-Generated Content Strategies

User-generated content (UGC) has become a core component of digital marketing strategies and plays a key role in driving business growth. As businesses navigate the ever-evolving landscape of digital marketing trends, leveraging UGC has proven to be an effective and cost-effective approach to connecting with audiences, building trust and improving brand visibility.

Introduction:

In the era of social media dominance, consumers are not mere spectators but active participants in the digital realm. User Generated Content means any content, whether images, videos, reviews or testimonials, created by users rather than by the brand itself. This organic content serves as a true reflection of the customer experience and can be used strategically to drive the business forward.

Why UGC matters:

1. Authenticity and Trustworthiness:

UGC gives a brand an authentic voice. Potential customers will trust the opinions and experiences of their peers more than traditional advertising. Reviews, testimonials and real stories shared by users create a sense of authenticity that resonates with audiences.

2. Engagement and Interaction:

Encouraging users to create content supports a two-way communication channel. Interactive campaigns, contests or challenges inspire users to actively engage with the brand. This not only increases brand awareness, but also creates a sense of community around the product or service.

3. Cost Effective Marketing:

Creating high quality content can be resource intensive. On the other hand, UGC is a cost-effective alternative. By harnessing the creativity of your audience, businesses can create a stream of diverse and engaging content without significant financial investment.

Implementation of UGC Strategies:

1. Social Media Platforms:

Leverage popular social media platforms where your target audience is most active. Encourage users to share their experiences through branded hashtags to create a digital tapestry of user stories.

2. Competitions and Challenges:

Design creative contests or challenges that challenge users to demonstrate their interaction with your product or service. This not only creates UGC but also fuels excitement and competition among participants.

3. Customer Reviews and References:

Actively seek and present customer reviews and testimonials on your website. This not only increases credibility, but also serves as valuable social proof for potential customers.

4. Influencer Collaboration:

Work with influencers who align with your brand. Influencers can create UGC that reaches a wider audience while providing a touch of credibility through their association with your product.

5. Interactive Content:

Create interactive polls, quizzes, or surveys that encourage user participation. This not only creates UGC, but also provides valuable insights into customer preferences and opinions.

Digital Marketing and UGC Trends:

1. Dominance of video content:

With the rise of short video content on platforms like TikTok and Instagram Reels, businesses can encourage users to create and share videos showcasing their brand experiences.

2. Personalization:

Customize UGC campaigns to match personalized marketing trends. Use data insights to understand user preferences and create content that resonates on an individual level.

3. Augmented Reality (AR) and Virtual Reality (VR):

Explore innovative ways to incorporate AR and VR into UGC strategies. Encourage users to create immersive experiences that bridge the digital and physical realms.

4. Social Commerce Integration:

As social commerce gains momentum, incorporate UGC into your eCommerce strategy. Present user reviews and images alongside product listings to enhance the shopping experience.

Measuring Success:

1. Engagement Metrics:
Track likes, shares, comments and overall engagement on UGC posts. Analyzing these metrics provides insight into the effectiveness of your UGC strategy.

2. Conversion rates:
See how UGC contributes to conversion rates. Analyze whether users who engage with UGC are more likely to convert into customers.

3. Brand Sentiment:
Gauge sentiment around UGC. Positive sentiment indicates that the content is resonating well with the audience, while negative sentiment can highlight areas for improvement.

4. Follower Growth:
Watch your social media followers grow during and after your UGC campaigns. An increase in the

number of followers indicates increased visibility and appeal of the brand.

In the dynamic environment of digital marketing, user-generated content is proving to be a powerful tool for business growth. By fostering authenticity, building trust and actively engaging with audiences, businesses can harness the potential of UGC to navigate emerging trends and create a strong digital presence. As technology continues to evolve, integrating UGC into digital marketing strategies will remain a key driver of sustainable business growth.

2.4 Content Personalization

Content personalization is a dynamic digital marketing strategy that plays a key role in driving business growth. In the ever-evolving online commerce environment, businesses are increasingly realizing the importance of tailoring their content to individual users. This approach not only improves user experience, but also significantly affects conversion rates and customer loyalty.

At its core, content personalization involves delivering targeted and relevant content to specific segments of your audience based on their preferences, behaviors and demographics. This personalization can happen across various digital channels such as websites, emails, social media and even advertisements. As businesses strive to stay ahead of the competitive digital market, integrating content personalization into their marketing strategies has become a key part of success.

One of the key benefits of content personalization is its ability to create a more engaging and personalized user experience. When users feel that the content they encounter is tailored to their interests and needs, they are more likely to engage and explore further. This personalized approach helps capture the user's attention amidst the vast amount of information available online and fosters a sense of connection between brand and consumer.

In the context of digital marketing trends, artificial intelligence (AI) and machine learning have emerged as powerful tools to effectively implement content personalization. These technologies allow businesses to analyze vast amounts of data, including user behavior, preferences and past interactions. By leveraging this data, marketers can develop algorithms that predict user preferences and deliver content that resonates with each individual.

Dynamic website personalization is a prime example of how businesses are using AI to personalize content. By analyzing user behavior in real time, websites can dynamically adjust their content, layout and recommendations to suit each visitor's preferences. This real-time adaptation improves the overall user experience and increases the likelihood of conversion.

Email marketing has also seen a transformation with the incorporation of content personalization. Instead of general mass emails, businesses now use user data to send targeted and relevant content to each subscriber. This not only improves open and click-through rates, but also strengthens the relationship between the brand and the consumer by providing content that aligns with their interests.

Social media platforms have become indispensable in the digital marketing landscape, and content personalization is extending its influence to these channels as well. Algorithms on platforms like Facebook and Instagram analyze user engagement patterns and deliver personalized content in user feeds. This customized content increases the chances of user interaction and encourages social sharing, thereby increasing the reach of the brand message.

Moreover, content personalization is not limited to pre-purchase interactions. Post-purchase engagement is just as important, and personalized content can play a significant role in customer retention. Personalized recommendations, exclusive offers and personalized post-purchase communications help build long-term customer relationships and strengthen brand loyalty.

The rise of content personalization is in line with consumers' growing expectations for personalized experiences. At a time when individuals are inundated with information, they appreciate brands that understand their preferences and provide content that adds value to their lives. This shift in consumer expectations has made content personalization not only a trend, but a necessity for businesses trying to stay relevant and competitive. As businesses continue to navigate the digital landscape, it is imperative to keep up with new trends. Content personalization is not a one-size-fits-all solution and its effectiveness depends on understanding your target audience, leveraging technology and constantly refining strategies based on data-driven insights. Implementing content personalization as part of a comprehensive digital marketing strategy enables businesses to not only survive, but thrive in the evolving digital ecosystem. In essence, it is the key to unlocking sustained business growth in an era where relevance and connectivity are paramount.

Chapter 3: Social Media Marketing Innovations

Social Media Marketing (SMM) has undergone significant changes in recent years and has become an indispensable part of digital marketing strategies. As businesses strive to grow in an ever-evolving digital environment, it is essential to stay abreast of the latest SMM innovations. In this comprehensive survey, we delve into the key trends and innovations in social media marketing that businesses can leverage for sustained growth.

1. Interactive Content: In an age of information overload, engaging content is paramount. Interactive content such as polls, quizzes and live videos have proven to be a powerful tool for increasing audience participation. Businesses are taking advantage of this trend to create more meaningful connections with target audiences,

foster increased brand loyalty and increase conversions.

2. Integrating Augmented Reality (AR): Integrating Augmented Reality into social media marketing is redefining user experiences. AR filters and features on platforms like Instagram and Snapchat allow businesses to offer immersive and entertaining content. This not only increases brand engagement, but also provides users with innovative ways to interact with products before making a purchase decision.

3. Ephemeral Content: The rise of ephemeral content on platforms like Instagram Stories and Snapchat has changed the dynamics of content consumption. Businesses use the temporary nature of these posts to create a sense of urgency and exclusivity and encourage real-time engagement. This trend is consistent with the shorter attention spans of modern consumers.

4. Social Commerce: The intersection of social media and e-commerce, known as social

commerce, represents a fundamental change for businesses. Platforms like Facebook and Instagram incorporate shopping features right into their interfaces, allowing users to make purchases without leaving the app. This seamless integration streamlines the customer journey and promotes higher conversions.

5. Chatbots and Messenger Marketing: Conversational marketing is gaining popularity through the use of chatbots and messaging apps. Businesses are integrating AI chatbots into social platforms to provide instant customer support, collect data and facilitate personalized interactions. Messenger marketing is proving to be an effective channel for direct communication and targeted promotion.

6. Cooperation with influencers: Influencer marketing is constantly evolving and companies are moving towards long-term cooperation with influencers who are in line with their brand values. Authenticity is key, and consumers are more likely

to trust recommendations from influencers who have made a real connection with their audience.

7. Video dominance: Video content remains at the forefront of SMM trends. Short videos, live broadcasts, and video storytelling are powerful tools for capturing and keeping your audience's attention. Platforms like TikTok have witnessed explosive growth and prompted businesses to adopt creative video strategies to showcase their products and services.

8. User Generated Content (UGC): The value of authentic user generated content cannot be overstated. Businesses encourage their audience to create content, whether through contests, challenges or referrals. UGC not only provides a diverse range of content, but also serves as social proof and increases brand credibility.

9. Privacy and Transparency: With growing concerns about privacy, businesses must prioritize transparency in their social media practices. Clear communication about data usage, respect for user

preferences and compliance helps build trust with audiences.

10. Emergence of niche platforms: While mainstream platforms continue to dominate, the emergence of niche platforms is a notable trend. Businesses are exploring opportunities on platforms that cater to specific interests or demographics, allowing for more targeted and personalized communications.

The social media marketing landscape is constantly evolving, presenting both challenges and opportunities for businesses. Embracing these innovations and maintaining adaptability is critical to harnessing the full potential of SMM in driving business growth. As we move forward, businesses that integrate these trends into their digital marketing strategies are likely to stand out in the competitive online space, foster stronger connections with their audiences, and achieve sustained growth.

3.1 Platform-specific Strategies (Facebook, Instagram, Twitter, LinkedIn, etc.)

Platform-specific strategies play a key role in the ever-evolving digital marketing landscape, offering businesses tailored approaches to engaging audiences across platforms. In this era of technological advancement, optimizing marketing strategies for each major platform such as Facebook, Instagram, Twitter and LinkedIn is essential for sustainable business growth.

1. Facebook: Social networking and targeted advertising:
Facebook remains a driving force in digital marketing thanks to its vast user base and robust advertising capabilities. Businesses can use Facebook's targeted advertising tools to reach specific demographics, interests and behaviors. Engaging content, including visually appealing images and videos, is essential on this platform to drive social engagement and improve brand visibility.

2. Instagram: Visual Storytelling and Influencer Collaboration:

Instagram, a visually focused platform, thrives on a compelling aesthetic. Businesses can harness the power of visual storytelling through high-quality images and videos. Working with influencers can greatly increase your reach because influencers authentically connect with their followers. Instagram Stories and Reels are valuable features for businesses that want to stay on top of digital marketing trends.

3. Twitter: Engage and leverage real-time trends:

Known for its real-time nature, Twitter provides a platform for businesses to instantly interact with their audience. Leveraging trending hashtags and participating in relevant conversations can increase visibility. Consistent and concise messaging is key on Twitter, where brevity often increases engagement. Brands can use Twitter to showcase their personality and respond promptly to customer inquiries.

4. LinkedIn: Professional Networking and Thought Leadership:

LinkedIn caters to a professional audience, making it ideal for B2B marketing and professional networking. Businesses can create thought leadership by sharing industry insights, whitepapers and participating in relevant groups. The platform's advertising capabilities enable targeted targeting of specific jobs, industries and company sizes, making it a valuable tool for business growth.

5. TikTok: Short video and creative expression:

As digital marketing trends evolve, platforms like TikTok are gaining in importance, especially among younger demographics. Short videos and creative expression are at the forefront on TikTok. Brands can take advantage of this platform by creating engaging and entertaining content that aligns with their brand identity. Working with TikTok influencers can further boost brand awareness.

6. Pinterest: Visual Discovery and Product Preview:

Pinterest is a visual discovery platform where users actively seek inspiration. Businesses can use

Pinterest to showcase products and services through visually appealing pins. The platform's shopping features enable a seamless transition from inspiration to purchase, making it a valuable asset for businesses in the e-commerce and creative industries.

7. Snapchat: FOMO Marketing and Interactive Content:

Known for its ephemeral content, Snapchat offers businesses an opportunity to capitalize on FOMO (Fear of Missing Out) marketing. Creating limited-time offers and exclusive content can increase engagement. The platform's interactive features, such as AR lenses, contribute to an immersive brand experience.

A successful digital marketing strategy involves understanding the unique characteristics of each platform and tailoring your content accordingly. Businesses that adopt platform-specific strategies can build a strong online presence, connect with their target audience, and stay ahead of evolving digital marketing trends for sustained growth in a competitive environment.

3.2 Influencer Marketing Trends

In the rapidly evolving digital marketing landscape, influencer marketing has proven to be an effective strategy for businesses seeking brand growth and visibility. As technology continues to shape consumer behavior, businesses must adapt to new trends to stay relevant. In this article, we'll explore the intersection of influencer marketing and digital marketing trends and highlight key strategies that can propel businesses to succeed in the ever-changing online landscape.

The rise of influencer marketing:

In recent years, influencer marketing has gained immense popularity and has become a cornerstone of digital marketing strategies for businesses across various industries. The concept is simple but powerful: use the influence of individuals with a significant and engaged following to promote products or services. This form of marketing has proven to be effective because of the trust and authenticity that influencers bring to the table.

Micro-influencers and niche markets:

One notable trend in influencer marketing is the growing focus on micro-influencers. These individuals may have a smaller following compared to mega influencers, but they often boast higher engagement rates and a more targeted audience. For businesses looking to tap into niche markets, working with micro-influencers can be particularly beneficial. Their authenticity and strong connection with their followers makes them strong brand advocates.

Authenticity and transparency:

As consumers become more discerning, authenticity and transparency have become integral to successful influencer marketing campaigns. Audiences are increasingly skeptical of overly polished and staged content and prefer real interaction. Businesses match their influencer collaborations with influencers who share the same values and resonate with their target audience, fostering a sense of authenticity that resonates with consumers.

Dominance of video content:

The rise of video content across various social media platforms has significantly impacted influencer marketing. Short videos on platforms like TikTok and Instagram Reels have become a popular medium for influencers to connect with their audience. Businesses are adapting by incorporating video content into their influencer campaigns, realizing its ability to capture attention and convey a message in a dynamic and engaging way.

Automation of influencer marketing:
As the influencer marketing landscape expands, businesses are turning to automation tools to streamline and scale their campaigns. Influencer marketing platforms enable businesses to identify suitable influencers, track campaign performance and effectively manage collaboration. Automation not only saves time, but also increases the accuracy of influencer selection and ensures that brands connect with influencers that truly resonate with their target audience.

Ephemeral content and stories:

The ephemeral nature of content on platforms like Instagram Stories and Snapchat has brought a sense of urgency to influencer marketing. Businesses are capitalizing on this trend by partnering with influencers to create limited-time promotions and exclusive content. The temporary nature of these posts promotes a sense of exclusivity and encourages followers to take immediate action, whether it's buying or participating in a campaign.

Integration with e-commerce:
Influencer marketing is increasingly linked to e-commerce strategies. Social commerce, where users can shop directly within social media platforms, is on the rise. Influencers play a key role in driving this trend by seamlessly integrating product recommendations and purchase links into their content. Businesses take advantage of this by providing influencers with unique discount codes and affiliate links, allowing them to track sales generated through collaboration with influencers.

Data-driven decision making:

The era of influencer marketing based solely on follower counts is giving way to more data-driven approaches. Businesses use analytics tools to evaluate the performance of influencer campaigns, measuring key metrics such as engagement rates, click-through rates, and conversion rates. This data-driven approach enables businesses to refine their strategies, optimize collaboration and maximize ROI from influencer marketing initiatives.

Diversity and Inclusivity of Influencers:
In response to calls for greater diversity and inclusivity in marketing, businesses are realizing the importance of working with influencers who represent a diverse range of backgrounds, cultures and perspectives. Inclusive influencer marketing not only reflects the diversity of the target audience, but also helps build a more authentic and engaging brand image.

The role of employee advocacy:
While influencers outside the company play a key role, businesses also leverage the influence of their own employees. Employee engagement programs

encourage employees to share company-related content on their personal social media accounts, organically extending brand reach. This approach humanizes the brand and uses the authenticity of employees to connect with a wider audience.

Influencer marketing is constantly evolving along with the dynamic landscape of digital marketing. Businesses that strategically embrace these trends can set themselves up for sustained growth and greater brand visibility. Whether it's working with micro-influencers, embracing authenticity, leveraging video content, or integrating influencer marketing with e-commerce, staying on top of these trends is critical to successfully navigating the ever-changing digital marketing landscape. As technology advances and consumer preferences evolve, businesses must remain agile in their approach to influencer marketing in order to harness its full potential for business growth.

3.3 Rise of Social Commerce

Social commerce has emerged as a key force in digital marketing, redefining the way businesses connect with consumers and drive growth. In recent years, the rise of social commerce has been nothing short of revolutionary, as platforms like Instagram, Facebook and Pinterest have evolved from mere social networks into robust e-commerce hubs. This transformation has significantly impacted digital marketing trends and offers businesses unique opportunities to engage their audience, build brand loyalty and ultimately increase sales.

At the heart of social commerce is the seamless integration of shopping experiences across social media platforms. This integration not only simplifies the consumer journey but also taps into the vast user base of these platforms. One of the key drivers behind the rise of social commerce is changing consumer behavior. Modern consumers, especially younger demographics, increasingly tend to discover, research and shop in the same digital space where they socialize and seek inspiration.

Digital marketing strategies have had to adapt to this shift, with businesses realizing the need to be present and active on social media platforms. Brands are no longer limited to traditional e-commerce websites; they now use social commerce features to showcase products, launch targeted advertising campaigns, and provide seamless shopping directly within users' social channels. This shift has become a cornerstone in strengthening brand-consumer relationships, as businesses can now interact with their audience in real-time, address queries and build a sense of community.

One of the significant advantages of social commerce lies in its ability to leverage user-generated content. Customers often share their experiences, reviews and even product recommendations on social media. Smart digital marketers use this user-generated content to build trust and authenticity for their brands. Integrating these recommendations into social commerce strategies provides real insights to potential customers, thereby influencing their purchasing decisions.

Additionally, the rise of social commerce has prompted a rethinking of influencer marketing. Influencers who have amassed a significant following on social media platforms now play a key role in digital marketing strategies. Brands work with influencers to promote their products through engaging and authentic content. This not only extends the brand's reach, but also leverages the influencer's credibility to drive conversions. The symbiotic relationship between influencers and brands has become a cornerstone of the social commerce landscape.

The role of data analytics in shaping social commerce strategies cannot be overstated. The amount of data generated by social media platforms allows businesses to gain deep insight into consumer behavior, preferences and trends. Digital marketers use this data to refine their targeting strategies, personalize content and optimize advertising campaigns. The result is a more tailored and effective approach to reaching the right audience at the right time.

As businesses continue to invest in social commerce, the integration of augmented reality (AR) and virtual reality (VR) technologies is coming to the fore. These immersive technologies enhance the online shopping experience by allowing users to virtually try on products or imagine them in a real-world environment. This not only adds a layer of interactivity but also reduces the uncertainty associated with online shopping, further increasing consumer confidence and conversion rates.

The rise of social commerce has also prompted a rethinking of traditional sales channels. The linear path from awareness to conversion has given way to a more dynamic and connected customer journey. Social commerce allows brands to reach consumers across multiple touchpoints to create a holistic brand experience. These developments require a shift in digital marketing strategies towards a multi-channel approach where online and offline aspects are seamlessly integrated to provide a cohesive brand experience.

Additionally, the integration of social commerce features into messaging apps has opened up new avenues for direct communication between businesses and consumers. Brands can now showcase products, provide customer support and even facilitate transactions within messaging platforms. This trend not only streamlines the shopping process, but is also in line with the preference for instant and convenient communication that is characteristic of the digital age.

The rise of social commerce has redefined the digital marketing landscape and offers unprecedented opportunities for businesses to grow. The seamless integration of shopping experiences across social media platforms, the power of user-generated content, collaboration with influencers, and the strategic use of data analytics are all tools for shaping effective social commerce strategies. As businesses continue to adapt to these trends, the synergy between social commerce and digital marketing will undoubtedly remain a driving force in driving brand success and sustained growth in the ever-evolving digital landscape.

Chapter 4: Data-Driven Decision Making

Data-driven decision making (DDDM) is a key component in digital marketing, playing a key role in shaping strategies and driving business growth. As the digital marketing landscape continues to evolve, businesses increasingly rely on data to make informed decisions and stay ahead of the competition. In this contextual survey, we delve into the importance of DDDM in the context of current digital marketing trends and explore how it contributes to business growth and success.

Understanding data-driven decision making:
Data-driven decision making involves using relevant data and insights to guide strategic decisions within an organization. In the context of digital marketing, this means using data to optimize campaigns, understand customer behavior and refine overall marketing strategies. The availability

of massive amounts of data, along with advanced analytical tools, has enabled businesses to move from gut feelings and intuition to a more scientific and accurate approach to decision-making.

The role of data in digital marketing trends:

1. Customer Personalization and Segmentation:

In the era of personalization, businesses are tailoring their marketing efforts to meet individual preferences. DDDM enables marketers to analyze customer data, understand preferences and create highly targeted campaigns. By providing personalized content to specific segments, businesses can increase customer engagement and build lasting relationships.

2. Integration of AI and Machine Learning:

Artificial intelligence (AI) and machine learning (ML) are changing digital marketing. DDDM harnesses the power of these technologies to analyze large data sets, predict consumer behavior, and automate marketing processes. This not only improves efficiency, but also enables real-time adjustments based on ongoing data analysis.

3. Multichannel Marketing Optimization:

As consumers interact across multiple channels, from social media to email to websites, DDDM is instrumental in optimizing multi-channel marketing efforts. Analyzing data from multiple touchpoints helps marketers understand the customer journey, allocate resources efficiently, and deliver a cohesive and seamless experience across channels.

4. Content Marketing Strategy:

Content remains the cornerstone of digital marketing and DDDM plays a key role in shaping content strategies. By analyzing content performance data, marketers can identify what resonates with their audience, refine the content creation process, and ensure that each piece of content contributes to overall business goals.

Implementation of data-driven decision making in digital marketing:

1. Collection and analysis of relevant data:

The first step in implementing DDDM is to collect and analyze relevant data. This includes customer demographics, behavior on digital platforms and engagement metrics. Tools like Google Analytics, social media analysis and customer relationship management (CRM) systems are invaluable for collecting and processing this data.

2. Setting clear goals:

Before you start analyzing data, it is essential to set clear marketing goals. Whether the goal is to increase brand awareness, increase website traffic, or increase sales, well-defined goals provide a framework for interpreting data and making decisions.

3. Use of advanced analytical tools:

Advanced analytics tools such as predictive analytics and customer journey mapping can provide deeper insights into consumer behavior. These tools go beyond basic data reporting to help marketers anticipate trends, identify patterns and make proactive decisions to stay ahead in a competitive digital landscape.

4. Experimentation and A/B testing:

DDDM promotes a culture of experimentation. Marketers can use A/B testing and other experimental methods to test different strategies and approaches. By analyzing the results, businesses can refine their tactics and ensure that marketing efforts are constantly optimized for maximum impact.

Case Studies: Example of DDDM Success in Digital Marketing:

1. Netflix:

Netflix is a prime example of a company using data to succeed in digital marketing. By analyzing user habits and preferences, Netflix recommends personalized content to engage users. This data-driven approach makes a significant contribution to customer retention and satisfaction.

2. Amazon:

Amazon's recommendation engine is a testament to the power of data driven decision making. By analyzing past purchases and browsing behavior, Amazon provides personalized product recommendations, improving the overall shopping experience and increasing sales.

3. Spotify:

Spotify uses data to create personalized playlists for users based on their listening history. This not only keeps users engaged with the platform, but also introduces them to new music, demonstrating the effectiveness of data-driven strategies in increasing user satisfaction and loyalty.

Challenges and Considerations in DDDM:

1. Privacy and compliance:

As businesses collect and analyze vast amounts of customer data, ensuring compliance with data protection regulations and addressing privacy concerns is critical. Marketers must find a balance between using data for statistics and respecting customer privacy.

2. Data quality and accuracy:

The success of DDDM depends on the quality and accuracy of the data analyzed. Inaccurate or incomplete data can lead to wrong decisions. It is essential to establish robust data collection processes and regularly review data quality.

3. Interpretation of data:

While advanced analytics tools provide valuable insights, interpreting data correctly is a skill marketers need to master. Misinterpretation can lead to wrong strategies. Investing in data literacy training for marketing teams can solve this problem.

4. Balancing data-driven and creative approaches:

While data provides valuable insights, there is a need to balance data-driven approaches with creative intuition. Relying too much on data alone can stifle innovation and the human touch in marketing campaigns.

The Future of DDDM in Digital Marketing:

As digital marketing continues to evolve, the role of DDDM will become increasingly prominent. The integration of emerging technologies such as augmented reality, virtual reality and the Internet of Things (IoT) will provide marketers with additional data points to leverage. Additionally, advances in data analytics and AI will enable marketers to make even more detailed decisions in real time.

In the dynamic environment of digital marketing, data-driven decision making is not just a strategy; it is a must. Businesses that adopt DDDM gain a competitive advantage by understanding their audience, optimizing campaigns, and adapting to ever-changing market trends. As we look to the future, the synergy between data and digital marketing will continue to drive innovation, support customer-centric approaches and ultimately contribute to sustainable business growth.

4.1 Role of Data in Marketing

In the ever-evolving landscape of digital marketing, data has proven to be the driving force behind successful strategies and sustainable business growth. Businesses today are inundated with vast amounts of data generated through various online channels, and effective use of this data can be a game-changer in the highly competitive digital market.

Understanding the Digital Marketing Landscape:
Digital marketing encompasses countless channels, from social media and email marketing to search engine optimization (SEO) and content marketing. In this diverse ecosystem, data serves as a compass that guides marketers in making informed decisions and optimizing their efforts for maximum impact.

Data as the basis of personalization:
One of the main trends in digital marketing is the increasing emphasis on personalization. Consumers now expect a customized experience, and data is the cornerstone on which personalization is built. Analyzing user behavior, preferences and demographics enables marketers to create targeted campaigns that resonate with specific audiences and foster a deeper connection between brand and consumer.

Decision support with Analytics:

Analytics tools play a key role in transforming raw data into useful insights. By leveraging analytics platforms, businesses can gain a comprehensive understanding of their audience's behavior, monitor the performance of marketing campaigns and identify areas for improvement. Real-time analytics further enable marketers to adapt their strategies on the fly, ensuring agility in a dynamic digital environment.

Customer Journey Mapping Improvements:
Digital marketing trends emphasize the importance of accurately mapping the customer journey. Data-driven insights allow businesses to identify touchpoints and interactions across different online platforms. This comprehensive understanding of the customer journey enables marketers to optimize each stage, providing a seamless and customized experience that leads to conversion.

Targeted advertising and retargeting:
With data, businesses can refine their advertising strategies to precisely target specific demographics. Social media platforms and search

engines offer advanced targeting capabilities and allow marketers to tailor their ads based on users' interests, demographics, and online behavior. In addition, retargeting campaigns use user data to re-reach individuals who have previously interacted with a brand, increasing the likelihood of conversion.

Optimization of SEO strategies:
Search engine optimization remains the cornerstone of digital marketing, and data plays a vital role in optimizing SEO strategies. By analyzing keywords, user search patterns, and competitor performance, businesses can improve their content to rank higher on search engine results pages. This data-driven approach ensures that digital content meets user intent, increases organic traffic and improves online visibility.

Effective email marketing through segmentation:
Email marketing continues to be a powerful tool for engaging with your audience. Data-driven segmentation allows businesses to categorize their audience based on specific criteria, ensuring email

content is relevant to each segment. This targeted approach significantly improves open rates, click-through rates and overall campaign effectiveness.

Measuring and Demonstrating ROI:
Demonstrating return on investment (ROI) is essential in digital marketing. The data allows marketers to track campaign performance, measure key performance indicators (KPIs) and accurately attribute conversions. This ability to quantify the impact of digital marketing efforts is critical to ensuring budget allocation and demonstrating the value of marketing initiatives to stakeholders.

Challenges and Ethical Considerations:
Although data has enormous potential, it also presents challenges and ethical considerations. Privacy concerns, data breaches and the need for transparent data practices are critical issues businesses must navigate. Finding a balance between using data for marketing purposes and

respecting consumer privacy is critical to building and maintaining trust.

In the digital age, data is not just a tool; it is the foundation upon which successful digital marketing strategies are built. Businesses that harness the power of data-driven insights gain competitive advantage, deliver personalized experiences, optimize campaigns and drive sustainable growth. As digital marketing trends continue to evolve, the role of data will remain central, shaping the future of marketing strategies and changing the way businesses connect with their audiences.

4.2 AI and Machine Learning in Marketing

Artificial intelligence and machine learning (ML) have become central elements in shaping the digital marketing landscape, driving business growth through data-driven strategies and personalized customer experiences. In this era of technological advancement, businesses that harness the power of AI and ML in their marketing efforts not only stay competitive, but also gain a significant advantage. This article explores the intersection of AI, ML and digital marketing trends and reveals the ways these technologies are driving business growth.

Understanding Artificial Intelligence and Machine Learning in Marketing:

1. Personalized customer experience:
AI and ML algorithms analyze vast amounts of customer data and enable businesses to create highly personalized experiences. By understanding individual preferences, buying behavior and engagement patterns, marketers can tailor their messages, recommendations and promotions. This not only increases customer satisfaction, but also increases the likelihood of conversion.

2. Predictive Analytics:
Machine learning algorithms allow marketers to predict future trends and consumer behavior based on historical data. This predictive analytics capability enables businesses to make informed decisions, optimize marketing campaigns and

allocate resources more efficiently. By anticipating market trends, businesses can stay ahead of the competition and adapt their strategies accordingly.

3. Chatbots and virtual assistants:
Chatbots and virtual assistants with artificial intelligence have become an integral part of customer service in digital marketing. These tools provide immediate answers to customer questions, streamline communication and increase user engagement. Additionally, they free up human resources and allow marketers to focus on more complex tasks while providing a seamless customer experience.

AI and ML in digital marketing trends

1. Hyper-personalization:
As customers demand more personalized experiences, hyper-personalization has become a major trend in digital marketing. AI and ML enable marketers to analyze customer data in real-time and deliver personalized content, product recommendations and promotions across multiple

channels. This level of customization increases customer engagement and loyalty.

2. Programmatic advertising:

Programmatic advertising uses artificial intelligence algorithms to automate the purchase of advertising space in real time. This automated approach ensures that ads are shown to the right audience at the right time, optimizing ad spend and increasing efficiency. Programmatic advertising is now the foundation of digital marketing strategies, providing targeted and relevant content to potential customers.

3. Voice search optimization:

With the increasing prevalence of voice-activated devices, optimizing for voice search has become essential. AI algorithms help understand natural language queries and allow businesses to tailor their content to match conversational search patterns. Voice search optimization is a digital marketing trend that ensures brands remain visible and accessible in an age of smart speakers and virtual assistants.

4. Customer Journey Mapping:

AI and ML are making significant contributions to understanding the customer journey. By analyzing touch points across different channels, companies can map the entire customer experience. This insight enables marketers to identify pain points, optimize touchpoints and create a seamless journey that increases customer satisfaction and loyalty.

5. Social Media Stats:

AI-driven tools analyze social media data to gain valuable insights into consumer sentiment, preferences and trends. Marketers can use these insights to improve their social media strategies, create content that resonates with their audience, and identify influencers who align with their brand. Social media analytics using artificial intelligence increase the effectiveness of digital marketing campaigns.

Case Studies: Real World Applications:

1. Amazon Referral Tool:

Amazon, a pioneer in e-commerce, uses a sophisticated recommendation engine powered by machine learning. By analyzing user behavior, purchase history and preferences, Amazon's algorithms suggest products that match individual tastes. This personalized approach contributes significantly to the platform's high conversion rates and customer satisfaction.

2. Netflix Content Recommendations:
Netflix uses machine learning algorithms to recommend content based on a user's viewing history and preferences. This personalized content delivery keeps subscribers engaged, reduces churn and contributes to the platform's success in the highly competitive streaming industry.

3. Personalized Spotify Playlists:
Spotify uses machine learning to create personalized playlists for its users. By analyzing listening habits, popular genres and user-created playlists, Spotify's algorithms provide a unique and enjoyable music experience. This personalization strategy increases user retention and satisfaction.

Overcoming challenges and ethical considerations: While AI and ML offer numerous advantages in digital marketing, there are issues and ethical considerations to navigate. Ensuring data privacy, avoiding algorithm distortions and maintaining transparency in processes controlled by artificial intelligence is paramount. Achieving a balance between personalization and respecting user privacy is critical to building trust and maintaining long-term customer relationships.

The future of AI and ML in digital marketing: Integrating AI and ML into digital marketing is an ever-evolving journey. As technology advances, new options and trends emerge. The future promises even more sophisticated applications, from improved chatbot interactions to advanced predictive analytics. Businesses that remain agile and embrace these innovations will continue to experience significant growth in the dynamic digital marketing landscape.

AI and ML have revolutionized digital marketing and offer unprecedented opportunities for businesses to grow. The ability to deliver hyper-personalized experiences, leverage predictive analytics, and adapt to evolving trends positions AI and ML as indispensable tools in the marketer's arsenal. By keeping up with new trends and ethical considerations, businesses can use these technologies to not only survive but thrive in the competitive realm of digital marketing.

4.3 Customer Data Privacy Concerns and Solutions

In the ever-evolving realm of digital marketing, where businesses use technology to connect with their audiences, protecting customer data has become a paramount concern. As businesses strive to grow in a digitally driven environment, they must navigate a delicate balance between using customer data for personalized marketing and respecting individuals' right to privacy.

Landscape of digital marketing trends:
Digital marketing has changed the way businesses reach and engage their target audience. From

social media advertising to email campaigns, the digital realm provides countless channels for businesses to connect with consumers. However, this increased reliance on digital platforms comes with its own set of challenges, central to which is the protection of customers' personal data.

Concerns about customer privacy:

Customers are increasingly aware of the value of their personal data. Data breaches and privacy scandals have raised concerns about how companies handle and protect sensitive information. The misuse or mishandling of customer data not only erodes trust, but can also lead to legal consequences and damage a brand's reputation.

One of the main problems is the unauthorized collection and sharing of personal data. Customers are concerned that their data may be sold to third parties or used without their consent. Additionally, the rise of sophisticated tracking technologies raises concerns about intrusive surveillance and the potential for data to be misused for purposes not originally intended by customers.

Striking a balance: Responsible use of customer data:

As businesses seek to leverage customer data for targeted marketing strategies, prioritizing transparency, consent and security is critical. Here are key solutions to address customer privacy issues in the digital marketing environment:

1. Transparent data collection procedures:
Businesses should clearly communicate their data collection practices to customers. This transparency builds trust and allows individuals to make informed decisions about sharing their information. Clearly written privacy policies, accessible terms of service and understandable consent mechanisms contribute to a more transparent relationship between businesses and their customers.

2. Opt-in consent mechanisms:

Rather than assuming consent, businesses should adopt explicit opt-in mechanisms. This means obtaining permission from customers before collecting and using their data for marketing purposes. Implementing robust opt-in processes ensures that individuals actively consent to the sharing of their information, promoting a sense of control and empowerment.

3. Data minimization:
Collecting only necessary data for marketing purposes, also known as data minimization, is a key principle of respecting customer privacy. By limiting the scope of data collection to what is necessary for targeted marketing, businesses reduce the risk of sensitive information being mishandled. This approach is privacy-by-design, where data protection is integrated into every stage of the marketing strategy.

4. Enhanced Data Security Measures;
To address concerns about data breaches and unauthorized access, businesses must prioritize robust security measures. Implementing encryption,

regularly updating security protocols and conducting thorough risk assessments contribute to the protection of customer data. Investing in cyber security not only protects customers, but also protects businesses from potential legal and financial consequences.

5. Giving customers control;

Giving customers control over their data is essential. Businesses can implement user-friendly dashboards or portals where individuals can manage their preferences, review collected data, and easily opt out of using specific data. This level of control not only respects individual privacy, but also improves the overall customer experience as customers have more control over their interactions with the brand.

The evolving regulatory landscape:

The digital marketing environment is not static, nor are regulations governing privacy. Governments around the world are adopting or updating legislation to strengthen consumer rights and hold businesses accountable for data protection. The

General Data Protection Regulation (GDPR) in Europe and the California Consumer Privacy Act (CCPA) in the United States are prime examples of this move towards expanded privacy regulations.

Adapting to regulatory changes:
Businesses operating in the digital space must keep up with evolving regulations and adapt their practices accordingly. This includes ongoing education and training of marketing teams to ensure compliance with new laws and standards. Proactively aligning marketing strategies with regulatory requirements not only mitigates legal risks, but also demonstrates a commitment to ethical data practices.

Building trust through ethical marketing practices:
Ultimately, the foundation of successful digital marketing is building and maintaining customer trust. By adopting ethical data practices and prioritizing customer privacy, businesses can differentiate themselves in a crowded marketplace. Trust is a valuable currency in the digital age, and

brands that prioritize privacy are more likely to build lasting relationships with their audiences.

The intersection of digital marketing trends and customer privacy requires a thoughtful and proactive approach on the part of businesses. Finding the right balance between using data for personalized marketing and respecting privacy is not only legal but also strategic. As technology continues to advance, businesses that prioritize transparent communication, consent, security and compliance will not only address current concerns, but also ensure continued growth in a dynamic digital environment.

Chapter 5: Emerging Technologies in Digital Marketing

Digital marketing has undergone a rapid transformation in recent years, fueled by the relentless evolution of technology. As businesses strive to stay ahead of the competitive landscape, keeping up with new technologies becomes paramount. In this era of constant change, understanding and adopting the latest digital marketing trends driven by innovative technologies can significantly impact business growth. This contextual content explores key new technologies in digital marketing and their role in shaping business expansion trends.

I Introduction to Digital Marketing Trends:
Digital marketing trends have become synonymous with business growth strategies. From social media

campaigns to search engine optimization, businesses use a variety of digital channels to connect with their target audience. However, with the advent of new technologies, the landscape is evolving, bringing both challenges and opportunities.

II. Artificial Intelligence (AI) and Machine Learning (ML) in Marketing:

AND. Personalization and customer statistics

Artificial intelligence and ML are revolutionizing the way businesses understand and interact with their audiences. These technologies enable hyper-personalization by analyzing vast amounts of data to predict consumer behavior. By providing personalized content and recommendations, businesses can improve the customer experience and strengthen brand loyalty.

B. Predictive analytics for targeted marketing

Predictive analytics based on AI and ML algorithms enable businesses to predict future trends and consumer preferences. This data-driven approach enables marketers to optimize their strategies, ensure more effective targeting and higher conversion rates.

III. Augmented Reality (AR) and Virtual Reality (VR) integration

AND. Immersive brand experiences
AR and VR are changing the way consumers interact with brands. By offering immersive experiences, businesses can create memorable brand interactions. For example, AR applications in retail allow customers to visualize products in their real-world environment before making a purchase decision.

B. Virtual shopping and try-on
E-commerce benefits greatly from AR and VR technologies, as customers can virtually try on products or experience a simulated shopping environment. This not only improves the online shopping experience, but also reduces the chances of product returns, which has a positive impact on business profitability.

IV. Chatbots and Conversational Marketing:

AND. 24/7 customer support

AI-powered chatbots are becoming an integral part of customer support. They provide immediate responses to customer inquiries and provide round-the-clock assistance. This not only improves customer satisfaction, but also streamlines the sales journey by guiding users through the decision-making process.

B. Conversation Shop

Conversational marketing uses chatbots and messaging apps to interact with customers in real time. Businesses can use this technology to guide users through the sales journey, answer questions and provide personalized recommendations, ultimately increasing conversion rates.

V. Voice Search Optimization (VSO):

AND. Change to search width

As voice-activated devices become ubiquitous, optimizing for voice search is critical. Businesses need to adapt their digital marketing strategies to meet conversational queries and focus on natural language and long-tail keywords.

B. Local SEO and voice-activated search:

Voice search has an impact on local businesses in particular. Optimizing for local SEO and tailoring content to answer location-specific queries ensures businesses are discoverable when users rely on voice-activated searches for nearby products or services.

VI. Blockchain technology in digital marketing:

AND. Transparent and secure transactions:

Blockchain technology ensures transparency and security in digital transactions. This is especially important in digital marketing where issues like ad fraud and lack of transparency are prevalent. Blockchain can verify digital ads, providing a secure and verifiable platform for advertisers and publishers.

B. Decentralized data ownership:

Blockchain gives users control over their data. This shift towards decentralized data ownership is in line with growing privacy concerns. Businesses adopting blockchain can build trust by assuring users that their data is safe and used responsibly.

VII. Social media trends and influencer marketing

AND. Rise of Short Content

Short content such as stories on platforms like Instagram and Snapchat continues to gain popularity. Businesses must adapt their content strategies to cater to shorter attention spans and create engaging and concise content that resonates with their audiences.

B. Micro and Nano Influencers

As influencer marketing matures, businesses are turning to micro and nano influencers to gain a more authentic connection with their audience. Leveraging influencers with smaller, dedicated followings can lead to higher engagement and more targeted reach.

Navigating the Future of Digital Marketing:

Staying ahead in the digital marketing landscape requires a proactive approach to adopting new technologies. From personalized experiences enabled by AI and ML to immersive interactions facilitated by AR and VR, businesses that embrace these trends are positioned for continued growth. As the digital marketing arena continues to evolve, the integration of innovative technologies will be key for businesses aiming to not only survive but thrive in the competitive digital space.

5. 1 Augmented Reality (AR) and Virtual Reality (VR)

In the ever-evolving digital marketing landscape, businesses are increasingly turning to immersive technologies such as augmented reality (AR) and virtual reality (VR) to engage their audiences and drive growth. These technologies are not just buzzwords, but powerful tools that can change the way businesses communicate with consumers. In this article, we explore the role of AR and VR in digital marketing trends and how they contribute to business growth.

1. Engaging Consumer Experiences:
AR and VR are redefining the consumer experience by offering immersive and interactive content. For businesses, creating engaging experiences is

critical to gaining and retaining the attention of their target audience. For example, AR overlays digital information onto the real world through mobile devices or AR glasses. This can be used for interactive ads that allow consumers to visualize products in their own environment before making a purchase decision.

VR, on the other hand, takes the user into a completely virtual environment. Businesses can use VR to create virtual showrooms or to simulate product experiences. This not only increases consumer engagement, but also builds a stronger emotional connection with the brand, fostering brand loyalty and repeat business.

2. Improved product visualization:

One of the significant challenges in digital marketing is to convey the true essence of a product. AR and VR provide solutions that allow customers to visualize products in a more realistic and interactive way. Using AR applications, customers can, for example, see how the furniture looks in their living room or how a pair of shoes complements their style. This not only improves the online shopping experience, but also reduces the likelihood of product returns as customers have a better understanding of what they are buying.

VR, with its immersive capabilities, allows customers to virtually experience products. For example, car manufacturers use VR to offer virtual test drives, allowing potential buyers to feel the driving experience without having to enter a physical showroom. This level of product visualization not only increases consumer confidence, but also differentiates businesses in a competitive market.

3. Personalized marketing campaigns:

AR and VR enable businesses to deliver highly personalized marketing campaigns. By analyzing user data and behavior, businesses can create AR experiences tailored to individual preferences. For example, AR apps can offer personalized recommendations based on previous user interactions to create a more personalized shopping experience.

VR takes personalization to the next level by immersing users in personalized virtual environments. Virtual spaces can be customized to reflect users' interests and preferences, making marketing messages more effective. Personalized AR and VR experiences not only increase engagement, but also contribute to higher conversion rates as customers feel a stronger connection with the brand.

4. Social media integration:

The integration of AR and VR into social media platforms has become a game-changer for digital marketing. Social media channels use these technologies to offer users more interactive and shareable content. AR filters and effects on platforms like Instagram and Snapchat allow businesses to create viral marketing campaigns that reach a wider audience.

VR can also be integrated into social media marketing strategies. Live streaming virtual events or creating immersive 360° videos can improve brand visibility and engagement on platforms like Facebook and YouTube. As social media continues to play a key role in digital marketing, businesses that use AR and VR technologies can stay ahead of the curve and reach a wider audience.

5. Data-driven statistics and analysis:
AR and VR in digital marketing provide valuable data and insights. Through user interactions with AR or VR applications, businesses can collect data about consumer behavior, preferences, and engagement patterns. Analyzing this data allows businesses to improve their marketing strategies, optimize content and deliver more targeted campaigns.

Additionally, data collected from AR and VR can contribute to a deeper understanding of customer preferences, allowing businesses to adapt and innovate based on real-time insights. This data-driven approach enables businesses to make informed decisions and increases the overall effectiveness of their digital marketing efforts.

Augmented reality and virtual reality are reshaping the digital marketing landscape by providing businesses with innovative ways to reach consumers. From immersive experiences to personalized campaigns and social media integration, AR and VR offer businesses a plethora of growth opportunities. As these technologies continue to evolve, businesses that use AR and VR in their digital marketing strategies are likely to stand out in a crowded market and foster lasting connections with their audiences. The future of digital marketing is undoubtedly linked to the immersive and transformative power of augmented reality and virtual reality.

5.2 Chatbots and Conversational Marketing

In the ever-evolving digital marketing landscape, businesses are constantly looking for innovative strategies to increase customer engagement and drive growth. Among the emerging trends, chatbots and conversational marketing have come to the fore, offering a dynamic approach to connecting with customers and prospects.

Understanding Chatbots:
Chatbots using artificial intelligence (AI) have become an integral part of online interactions with

customers. These virtual assistants simulate human conversations and provide immediate answers to users' questions. Their efficiency in handling routine tasks, answering frequently asked questions and guiding users through processes has made them a valuable asset to businesses in various industries.

In the context of digital marketing, Chatbots serve as a 24/7 customer support channel that ensures quick assistance and improves the overall user experience. They make communication more efficient, shorten response times and increase customer satisfaction. Additionally, chatbots can be integrated into websites, social media platforms, and messaging apps, allowing users a seamless omnichannel experience.

The Rise of Conversational Marketing:

Conversational marketing takes a more proactive approach by using one-to-one connections between marketers and customers in real time. It uses chat-based interactions to drive engagement, capture valuable insights, and guide users through the buyer's journey. Unlike traditional marketing methods, conversational marketing focuses on personalized, interactive conversations that align with individual user preferences.

One notable aspect of conversational marketing is the use of messaging apps. With the growing popularity of platforms like WhatsApp, Facebook Messenger and Slack, businesses are looking for new ways to reach and engage their target audience. These messaging apps provide a direct and intimate channel for communication and allow brands to deliver customized content and promotions.

Digital Marketing Trends Shaping the Future:

1. Personalization: Chatbots and conversational marketing thrive on personalization. By analyzing user behavior and preferences, businesses can tailor their marketing messages, offers and recommendations to create a more personalized and relevant experience for each customer.

2. Data-Driven Insights: Data generated through Chatbot interactions and conversational marketing provides valuable insights into customer behavior. Marketers can use this data to refine their strategies, understand customer needs, and make informed decisions for targeted campaigns.

3. User Engagement: Traditional marketing methods often struggle to get and keep users' attention. However, chatbots and conversational marketing offer a more engaging and interactive experience, keeping users engaged and interested in the brand's message.

4. Automation for Efficiency: Automation is a key part of both chatbots and conversational marketing. Automating routine tasks not only increases efficiency, but also frees up resources for more strategic marketing initiatives. This automation is especially beneficial when handling high-volume, repetitive customer inquiries.

5. Availability 24/7: One of the significant advantages of Chatbots is their 24/7 availability.

This ensures that businesses can cater to a global audience regardless of time zones and provide timely information and assistance.

Implementation of chatbots and conversational marketing strategies:

1. Define Goals: Clearly outline the goals of incorporating chatbots and conversational marketing into your digital strategy. Whether it's improving customer support, increasing sales, or gathering feedback, a well-defined purpose will drive the implementation process.

2. User-Centric Design: Develop chatbots with a user-centric approach. The flow of the conversation should feel natural and the user interface should be intuitive. A positive user experience contributes to increased customer engagement and satisfaction.

3. Cross-Channel Integration: Ensure seamless integration of chatbots and conversational marketing across multiple digital channels. Consistency in messaging and branding helps in

reinforcing brand identity and creating a unified customer experience.

4. Data Security: Due to the nature of personal interactions, prioritize data security. Implement robust measures to protect user information and ensure compliance with data protection regulations.

5. Continuous Improvement: Monitor and analyze the performance of chatbots and conversational marketing. Regularly update and refine conversation scripts based on user feedback and changing market dynamics.

As businesses navigate the digital landscape, the adoption of chatbots and conversational marketing is emerging as a transformational strategy for achieving sustainable growth. By fostering personalized interactions, leveraging data-driven insights and embracing automation, businesses can create a more responsive and engaging digital presence. The future of digital marketing undoubtedly involves a conversational approach, and those who embrace it are likely to stay ahead of the competition and create a stronger connection with their audience.

5.3 Voice Search Optimization

Voice Search Optimization (VSO) has emerged as a key aspect of digital marketing that significantly impacts businesses and their growth strategies. As technology evolves, consumer behavior undergoes transformations and businesses must adapt to stay relevant. In this context, understanding the nuances of voice search optimization is critical to harnessing its potential in the ever-changing digital marketing landscape.

Introduction

The proliferation of voice-activated devices and virtual assistants in recent years has pushed voice search into the mainstream. As smart speakers, smartphones, and other connected devices become ubiquitous, users increasingly rely on voice commands to search for information, ask questions, and perform various tasks. This shift in user behavior has profound implications for businesses and requires a strategic approach to voice search optimization.

The Rise of Voice Search:
Voice search has gained popularity due to its convenience and speed. Users can simply speak their questions and the device will respond with relevant information. This natural and hands-free interaction has changed the way people access information, and businesses need to recognize this shift to ensure they remain visible to their target audience.

Impact on Search Engine Optimization (SEO):
Traditional SEO practices are no longer sufficient in a voice-controlled landscape. Voice searches often differ from text queries because they are more conversational and long. As a result, businesses must adapt their SEO strategies to accommodate these nuances. Long-tail keywords, natural language content, and local optimization are critical components of a successful voice search optimization strategy.

Understanding User Intent:
One of the key challenges of voice search optimization is accurately understanding user intent. Voice search tends to be more contextual and requires businesses to anticipate user needs and tailor their content to them. Analyzing the conversational nature of voice queries helps in creating content that aligns with user intent, ultimately increasing the chances of appearing in voice search results.

Local Search Optimization:
Voice search often has a strong local intent, with users looking for information about nearby businesses, services or products. Local search optimization is therefore an integral part of a comprehensive voice search optimization strategy. Businesses should ensure that their online profiles, such as Google My Business, are up-to-date and contain accurate information so that voice-enabled devices can more easily provide relevant local results.

Role of Selected Excerpts:

Voice search results often rely heavily on featured snippets – short, informative snippets displayed at the top of search engine results. Structuring your content to answer common business-related questions can increase your chances of appearing in these snippets and improve your visibility in voice search results.

Adapting content for voice:
Creating content that resonates with voice search requires understanding the natural language patterns that users use when talking to virtual assistants. Businesses should focus on creating conversational and concise content that directly addresses user queries. This approach not only improves the visibility of voice search results, but also improves the overall user experience.

Optimized for mobile and voice search:
Since a significant portion of voice search takes place on mobile devices, optimizing your website for mobile is inherently linked to effective voice search optimization. Mobile-friendly websites with fast loading and responsive design contribute to the

smooth use of voice search, which has a positive impact on the online visibility of the business.

Development of virtual assistants:
As virtual assistants continue to evolve, incorporating artificial intelligence and machine learning capabilities, the accuracy and sophistication of voice search results will increase. Businesses should keep up with these developments and be prepared to adapt their voice search optimization strategies accordingly.

Analytics and measurement.
Measuring the effectiveness of voice search optimization efforts is critical to refining strategies and staying ahead in a competitive digital environment. Analytics tools can provide insight into voice search keyword performance, user behavior and impact on overall website traffic. This data-driven approach enables businesses to make informed decisions and optimize their content for better results.

Voice search optimization is not just a trend, but a fundamental shift in how users access information online. Businesses that recognize the importance of voice search and proactively adapt their digital marketing strategies will gain a competitive advantage in reaching and engaging their target audience. Embracing the complexity of voice search, from understanding user intent to optimizing content for natural language, is paramount to continued growth in the dynamic field of digital marketing. As technology continues to evolve, businesses that prioritize voice search optimization will be better positioned to navigate the digital landscape and capitalize on new opportunities for business growth.

Chapter 6: Future Outlook and Actionable Insights

The future outlook of digital marketing trends holds huge promise for businesses seeking sustainable growth in an increasingly competitive environment. As technology continues to evolve, marketers are presented with new opportunities and challenges that require strategic approach and adaptability. In this era of digital transformation, staying ahead requires not only an understanding of emerging trends, but also the ability to derive useful insights from them. Let's explore some key digital marketing trends and actionable insights businesses can use to drive growth.

Dominance of content marketing:
Content remains king in digital marketing and is expected to grow in importance. Businesses must focus on creating valuable, relevant and engaging

content that resonates with their target audience. Video content in particular continues to gain popularity and businesses should invest in high-quality video production to enhance brand storytelling.

Actionable Insight: Create a comprehensive content strategy that aligns with your brand values and resonates with your audience. Use video content to increase engagement and connect with consumers on a more personal level.

Personalization based on artificial intelligence:
Artificial intelligence (AI) is revolutionizing digital marketing by enabling hyper-personalized experiences. Artificial intelligence algorithms analyze vast amounts of data to understand consumer behavior, preferences and patterns, enabling businesses to deliver targeted and relevant content. Personalization not only increases customer satisfaction, but also increases conversion rates.

Actionable Insight: Implement AI-based tools to analyze customer data and create personalized marketing campaigns. Tailor content, recommendations and offers based on individual preferences to create a more personalized and engaging customer experience.

Voice search optimization:
With the rise of virtual assistants and smart speakers, voice search is becoming increasingly prevalent. Optimizing digital content for voice search is essential for businesses that want to stay visible in search engine results. Voice search queries are often conversational and require a change in keyword strategy and content optimization.

Actionable Insight: Conduct in-depth keyword research to identify and integrate long and conversational phrases. Optimize website content for voice search by providing concise and informative answers to common questions related to your industry.

Social commerce integration:

Social media platforms are evolving beyond just brand awareness and engagement. Integrating e-commerce features directly into social media channels is a growing trend. Businesses can now sell products directly through platforms like Instagram and Facebook, giving users a seamless shopping experience.

Actionable Insight: Explore social commerce opportunities by setting up and optimizing online stores on relevant social media platforms. Use social media advertising to promote products and drive conversions directly from social channels.

Privacy and trust:

As digital marketing becomes more sophisticated, consumers are increasingly concerned about the protection of personal data. Trust is a critical factor in building and maintaining customer relationships. Businesses must prioritize transparent data practices and comply with regulations to strengthen the trust of their audience.

Action Insights: Clearly communicate your privacy policy to customers. Implement robust security measures and comply with relevant data protection regulations. Building trust through transparent practices can lead to increased customer loyalty and positive brand perception.

Augmented Reality (AR) Experience.

AR is changing the way consumers interact with products and services. Businesses can use AR to provide immersive and interactive experiences, especially in industries such as retail and e-commerce. Virtual try-ons, product visualizations and interactive ads enhance the customer experience and increase engagement.

Actionable Insight: Explore opportunities to integrate RR experience into your marketing strategy. Create AR-based campaigns that allow customers to interact with your products in a virtual space, providing a unique and memorable brand experience.

Sustainability and social responsibility:

Consumers are increasingly aware of environmental and social issues and expect the brands they support to share these values. Incorporating sustainability and social responsibility into digital marketing strategies can improve brand reputation and attract socially conscious consumers.

Actionable Insight: Show your commitment to sustainability and social responsibility in your marketing messages. Emphasize green practices, community involvement and ethical sourcing to resonate with consumers who prioritize these values.

The future of digital marketing holds enormous potential for businesses that embrace new trends and utilize useful insights. By focusing on content marketing, AI-based personalization, optimizing for voice search, integrating social commerce, prioritizing privacy, exploring AR experiences, and incorporating sustainability, businesses can position themselves for continued growth in a dynamic digital environment. Stay agile, constantly analyze performance metrics and adapt strategies to stay ahead in the ever-evolving world of digital marketing.

6.1 Predictions for the Future of Digital Marketing

The field of digital marketing is constantly evolving, driven by technological advancements and changing consumer behavior. Looking ahead, several trends are poised to shape the field of digital marketing and play a key role in driving business growth.

Artificial Intelligence (AI) is set to revolutionize digital marketing strategies. Machine learning algorithms can analyze vast amounts of data to understand consumer preferences and behavior, enabling businesses to deliver personalized and targeted content. From chatbots providing instant customer support to predictive analytics driving marketing decisions, AI is becoming a cornerstone for businesses looking to stay competitive in the digital space.

Voice search is another frontier that digital marketers must embrace. With the increasing prevalence of smart speakers and virtual assistants, optimizing content for voice queries becomes essential. Businesses must adapt their SEO strategies to accommodate natural language and conversational queries and ensure visibility in voice search results.

Video content is already a powerful tool today and is expected to grow in importance. With short videos gaining popularity on platforms like TikTok and Instagram Reels, it is essential for marketers to incorporate engaging video content into their campaigns. Live broadcasts, virtual events and interactive videos will further enhance user engagement and brand visibility.

Social media remains the driving force behind digital marketing, but the way it is used is evolving. Brands focus on creating authentic connections with their audiences through meaningful content and community building efforts. Additionally, the rise of social commerce allows businesses to sell products directly through social media platforms, simplifying the customer journey and enhancing the shopping experience.

Personalization is key in the future of digital marketing. Consumers expect personalized experiences, and businesses that can deliver relevant content based on individual preferences will stand out. Leveraging customer data analytics and insights will enable marketers to create hyper-targeted campaigns, foster stronger connections and increase conversion rates.

The Internet of Things (IoT) is creating new opportunities for digital marketers. As more devices connect, marketers can collect real-time data to understand user behavior and preferences. This data can inform personalized marketing strategies and deliver messages at the right time and through the right channels.

Privacy concerns are shaping the future of digital marketing regulation. With stricter data protection laws such as GDPR and CCPA, businesses must prioritize transparent data practices and ensure compliance. Building consumer trust in the use of data is paramount to maintaining positive brand relationships.

Augmented Reality (AR) and Virtual Reality (VR) are gaining ground in digital marketing, offering immersive experiences to consumers. From virtual trial experiences for retail products to AR-enhanced advertisements, these technologies create memorable interactions and leave a lasting impact on audiences.

The future of digital marketing offers exciting opportunities for business growth. By embracing artificial intelligence, optimizing for voice search, leveraging video content, mastering social media strategies, prioritizing personalization, leveraging IoT data, navigating privacy issues, and exploring AR and VR, businesses can stay ahead of the ever-evolving digital landscape. . Staying adaptive and innovative in these areas will be critical to success in the dynamic world of digital marketing.

6.2 Strategies for Adapting to Ongoing Changes

In the fast-paced field of digital marketing, staying ahead of the curve is paramount to business growth. The landscape is constantly evolving and new technologies, consumer behavior and algorithms are shaping the way brands connect with their audiences. Adapting to ongoing change requires a strategic approach that includes innovation and flexibility. Here are key strategies for businesses looking to navigate and thrive within digital marketing trends.

1. Continuous learning and skill development:
Digital marketing is dynamic and being informed is essential. Invest in the continuous learning of your team to keep up with new trends, tools and platforms. This may include attending industry conferences, participating in webinars, or enrolling in relevant online courses. A well-informed team is better equipped to design strategies that resonate with the latest digital marketing dynamics.

2. Make data-driven decisions:

Harness the power of data analytics to gain insight into consumer behavior and campaign performance. Use analytics tools to track key metrics, understand customer preferences, and optimize marketing strategies accordingly. Data-driven decision-making not only increases the effectiveness of campaigns, but also enables rapid adjustments based on real-time feedback.

3. Agile marketing strategies:

In a fast-changing digital environment, rigid marketing plans can stop working before implementation. Adopt agile methodologies that emphasize flexibility and quick adjustments. Regularly review your marketing strategies and enable quick pivots based on performance data and market shifts. An agile approach allows businesses to quickly respond to emerging trends and consumer demands.

4. Take advantage of emerging technologies:

Explore and incorporate new technologies into your digital marketing arsenal. Artificial intelligence (AI), augmented reality (AR) and chatbots are just a few examples that can revolutionize customer engagement and campaign optimization. Staying ahead in digital marketing means experimenting with cutting-edge technologies to gain a competitive edge.

5. Improve your social media presence:

Social media is the cornerstone of digital marketing and its dynamics are constantly changing. Stay up to date with the latest features and algorithms on platforms like Facebook, Instagram, Twitter and LinkedIn. Engage your audience through interactive content, live videos and stories. Building a strong social media presence and adapting to platform changes is essential to maintaining a vibrant online community.

6. Prioritize mobile optimization:

As mobile usage continues to rise, it is imperative to ensure that your digital marketing strategies are mobile-friendly. Optimize websites, emails and ads for a seamless mobile experience. This not only caters to the growing mobile audience, but also aligns with search engine algorithms that favor mobile-friendly content.

7. Support customer-centric approaches:

The customer should be at the heart of every digital marketing strategy. Adapt to changing consumer preferences by proactively seeking feedback, monitoring reviews, and responding to customer inquiries. Personalization and customization are key trends, so tailor your marketing messages to resonate with your audience on a more individual level.

The digital marketing landscape is constantly changing. To ensure business growth, it is essential to embrace change rather than resist it. By fostering a culture of continuous learning, data-driven decision-making, and technological innovation, businesses can not only adapt to ongoing change, but also position themselves as leaders in the dynamic world of digital marketing.

6.3 Case Studies on Successful Implementations

Successful implementations of digital marketing strategies have become integral for businesses seeking growth in today's dynamic environment. Through case studies, we can learn how organizations are using new trends to improve their online presence, engage audiences and increase revenue.

One notable case is that of a retail giant that adopted influencer marketing to increase its digital footprint. By working with influencers who resonated with their target audience, the company saw a substantial increase in brand awareness and customer engagement. Authentic endorsements from influencers helped create a connection with consumers, which translated into better sales and loyalty.

In another case, a tech startup capitalized on the growing trend of video content. The company recognized the power of platforms like YouTube and TikTok and created engaging and informative videos showcasing its products. This not only attracted a wider audience but also increased the credibility of the brand as an expert in the field. The success of this approach was evident in the increase in website traffic and conversion rates.

Often considered a traditional tool, email marketing has played a key role in the success story of e-commerce businesses. By adopting personalized and targeted email campaigns, the company effectively nurtured leads and retained customers. Strategic use of data-driven insights ensured that every communication resonated with the recipient, leading to increased customer lifetime value and repeat business.

Furthermore, the integration of artificial intelligence (AI) into digital marketing strategies has yielded remarkable results for various organizations. One case study involves a financial services company that implemented AI-driven chatbots to improve customer interaction. These chatbots not only provided instant support but also collected valuable data about customer preferences. Insights gained from AI analytics have allowed the company to improve its marketing strategies, leading to significant increases in customer satisfaction and retention.

Social media continues to change the digital marketing game. The global fashion brand has harnessed the power of social platforms to create immersive and shareable content. By aligning with trending topics and using visually appealing posts, the brand has cultivated a devoted online community. This not only strengthened the brand presence but also led to a surge in online sales and brand advocacy.

Search Engine Optimization (SEO) remains the cornerstone of digital marketing success, as evidenced by a regional service provider. Through a comprehensive SEO strategy, the company has ensured that its website ranks high in relevant searches. This increased online visibility translated into a higher flow of organic traffic, generating more leads and conversions.

Additionally, the adoption of data analytics tools has enabled businesses to make informed decisions. The software company used the potential of analytics to track user behavior on its website and in the app. By understanding customer journeys, the company optimized its digital marketing campaigns, resulting in improved user experience and higher conversion rates.

The success stories derived from the case studies underscore the importance of adopting digital marketing trends for sustainable business growth. Whether through collaboration with influencers, video content, personalized email campaigns, AI integration, social media engagement, SEO strategies or data analytics, organizations can adapt their approaches to align with evolving consumer behavior. By remaining agile and innovative, businesses can effectively navigate the digital landscape and carve out a path to success in an increasingly competitive market.

Conclusion

Digital marketing trends play a key role in shaping the environment for business growth and provide companies with innovative strategies to reach and engage their target audience. In this analysis, we have explored several key trends that have dominated the digital marketing arena and offered insight into their impact on business expansion.

The advent of social media marketing has changed the game, allowing businesses to connect with their audiences on a personal level. Platforms like Facebook, Instagram and Twitter have become indispensable tools for building a brand and interacting with customers. Harnessing the power of influencer marketing on these platforms has further boosted brand visibility and credibility, proving to be a trend of enduring importance.

Additionally, the rise of video marketing has changed the way businesses communicate their messages. With the growing popularity of platforms like YouTube and TikTok, video content has become the preferred medium to capture consumer attention. Short videos, in particular, have gained enormous popularity, requiring businesses to adapt their content strategies to meet the preferences of modern audiences.

Search Engine Optimization (SEO) remains a cornerstone of digital marketing and its evolution has been marked by the changing algorithms of the major search engines. Keeping up with these algorithmic shifts is essential for businesses that want to maintain a strong online presence. The integration of artificial intelligence and machine learning into SEO has added a new level of complexity that requires marketers to adopt data-driven approaches to improve website visibility and user experience.

Email marketing, despite being one of the oldest forms of digital marketing, is constantly evolving. Personalization and automation are key trends in this area, enabling businesses to deliver targeted and timely messages to their audiences. The importance of building and maintaining email subscriber lists cannot be overstated as it provides a direct channel to communicate and build relationships with potential and existing customers. The emergence of chatbots and conversational marketing has simplified customer interactions and provided instant support and information. Integrating chatbots into websites and messaging apps has become the norm, improving the user experience and freeing up human resources for more complex tasks. As AI continues to advance, we can expect further improvements in chatbot capabilities, making them an integral part of customer engagement strategies.

The importance of data analytics in digital marketing cannot be ignored. The ability to collect, analyze and derive useful insights from data has become a competitive advantage. Businesses that harness the power of analytics gain a deeper understanding of customer behavior, allowing them to tailor their marketing efforts for maximum impact. The rise of big data and advanced analytics tools has democratized data-driven decision-making, allowing even small businesses to reap the benefits of data analytics.

Mobile marketing has grown exponentially due to the increasing use of smartphones. Optimizing your website and content for mobile devices is no longer an option, but a necessity. Integrating location-based marketing and using mobile apps to engage customers have become standard practices. As mobile technology continues to grow, businesses must prioritize mobile-friendly strategies to stay relevant in the marketplace.

The concept of user-generated content has come to the fore as consumers increasingly rely on reviews and recommendations from their peers. Encouraging and showcasing user-generated content not only builds trust, but also creates a sense of community around the brand. Businesses that actively engage their customers in the content creation process foster stronger connections, foster loyalty and support.

The ever-evolving nature of digital marketing requires an agile approach. Businesses that adapt quickly to new trends and consumer behavior are more likely to thrive in the digital environment. However, it is essential to strike a balance between embracing new trends and maintaining consistency in core marketing principles.

The dynamic nature of digital marketing trends continues to shape the growth strategies of businesses worldwide. From social media and video marketing to AI-driven analytics and mobile optimization, staying ahead of the curve is critical to continued success. Looking to the future, the integration of technology, data-driven insights and a customer-centric approach will remain at the forefront of effective digital marketing strategies, giving businesses the tools they need to not only survive but thrive in a competitive environment. online environment.